Praise for Navigating Intimacy

"A timely, necessary guide to integrating sex therapy into couples work. Full of practical tools to aid therapists in gaining insight and knowledge. It is truly essential reading for couples and sex therapists."

—**Cassandra Aasmundsen-Fry, PsyD,** clinical psychologist, founder of MindWell, and author of *The Glory in Us All*

"*Navigating Intimacy* by Dr. Isabelle Morley and Dr. Bailey Hanek is a gem for anyone looking to deepen their understanding of couples and sex therapy. I wish I'd had this book earlier in my career—it fills a major gap with its perfect blend of research, relatable insights, and practical tools. Whether you're a professional or simply curious about fostering healthier relationships, this guide makes complex topics approachable and engaging. It's an invaluable resource I'll be turning to again and again."

—**Rebecca Eudy, LMFT,** AASECT- and EFT-certified, cohost of *The Love Lab Uncensored* podcast

"In this day of widening appreciation for the many forms of sexual identities and gender variation, Isabelle Morley and Bailey Hanek put the integration of intimacy and sexuality front and center in their work with couples. With unflinching directness and accessibility, they make couples work both comprehensible and brave. Without shying away from incisive language, they look at the 'negative cycles' that plague couples and those therapists who want to treat them, mapping out the many challenges in this terrain in practical yet substantive ways.

This book fills many gaps in the training of therapists where couples work is usually seen as a specialty, often mistakenly dividing couples work from sex therapy. In contrast, Morley and Hanek imply a definition of healthy relating: strong emotional connection, sound communication, conflict resolution skills, and sexual freedom ('sex positivity'). Who would argue with these? They propose an integration of all of these areas with this most accessible and comprehensive guide that promises to deepen intimacy in all its forms. All therapists, trainees, and consumers of couples' treatment would benefit greatly from reading this book and using it throughout their lifetime in both professional and personal domains."

—**Andrea Celenza, PhD,** author of *Erotic Transferences* and *Transference, Love, Being*

NAVIGATING INTIMACY

An Introductory Guide to Couples and Sex Therapy

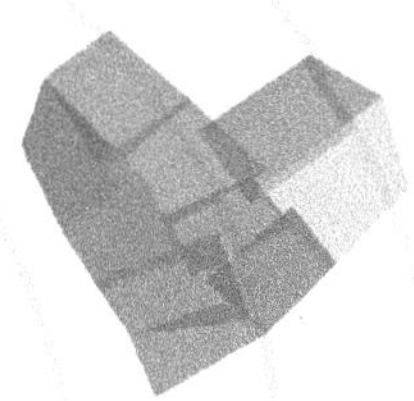

Isabelle Morley, PsyD • Bailey Hanek, PsyD

NAVIGATING INTIMACY

Published by
PESI Publishing, Inc.
3839 White Ave
Eau Claire, WI 54703

Cover and interior design by Amy Rubenzer
Editing by Chelsea Thompson

ISBN 9781683737995 (print)
ISBN 9781683738008 (ePUB)
ISBN 9781683738015 (ePDF)

This book is dedicated to the hard-working, knowledge-hungry therapists who continually strive to provide the best care possible.

And to the couples of the world, who know that strong relationships require work, and are willing to do it.

Table of Contents

Introduction

Romantic relationships are an almost universal human experience that can be a powerful source of happiness and meaning. They also come with many unique challenges, such as attachment issues, communication and conflict resolution deficits, and a poor understanding of or stigma about sexuality. These challenges make it easy for couples to fall into negative cycles, despite their best intentions and even when they make genuine efforts to change. Breaking out of these ineffective patterns requires the help of skilled clinicians.

Unfortunately, there are many barriers to accessing help, particularly for historically underserved communities. Even when a couple overcomes the financial and structural hurdles to access a therapist, there is no guarantee that the therapist is competent in working with couples. Despite the reality that romantic relationships affect the vast majority of people, working with couples is not a compulsory course for most graduate programs, which means most therapists do not receive sufficient training in how to do it. Without a solid foundation of knowledge, many therapists apply the same principles and practices they have learned for working with individuals to the couples on their caseload. This approach is typically ineffective at best, and destructive at worst.

Even therapists who are willing to pursue additional postgraduate training in order to properly treat couples will face challenges. The first challenge is deciding where exactly to start. There are many effective and evidence-based approaches for working with couples, each with its own specific training and certification path. A second challenge is the substantial investment of time and finances involved in further training. Third, therapists who may not want to pursue this as a specialty but are interested in learning more don't know the best place to gain a broader understanding of the work.

We designed this book as a concise yet comprehensive overview of relationship treatment principles as well as encouragement and resources for therapists to learn more, in the hope of equipping and encouraging more clinicians to become qualified and comfortable with addressing both the romantic and sexual aspects of relationships with clients. However, our main reason for writing this book is to correct a crucial flaw in the field of psychotherapy: that couples therapy and sex therapy are taught separately. This puts clinicians in the position of having to choose one over the other—should they pursue training on how to strengthen emotional connection, communicate better, and resolve recurring conflicts, or should they seek education on how to help couples talk about and navigate sexual challenges?

Our contention, supported by a combined twenty years of practice and research, is that these two paths overlap—that couples therapy and sex therapy should be integrated. After all, it's rare for couples to experience sexual problems without also having difficulty communicating. Likewise, most couples seeking therapy to resolve disconnection and unhappiness also struggle with a lack of sexual intimacy.

Ideally then, clinicians working with couples should obtain comprehensive training that covers both areas. Instead, they are largely left to figure out their own training path—one that may or may not include all they need to know.

Because of these significant challenges to clinicians receiving adequate training, it is common for couples to try couples or sex therapy and report that it "didn't help." Couples often say that the therapy is too unstructured and becomes just another space for them to fight and misunderstand each other. Many say that therapy isn't a safe space, that clinicians seem uncomfortable with the content (especially when it was about sexuality), or that it feels like "no one was in charge." Perseverant couples will try again with another therapist (or several) until they find the right fit, but others will become discouraged by the experience and, to the detriment of their relationship, stop the search for further help.

Investing the time and money into therapy is not done lightly for most couples. They are sacrificing to work on their relationship, and they need to trust that their therapist can help them. Some partners are anxious about couples work, while others feel ambivalent or resistant toward it, even as they agree to a first session. It is deeply vulnerable to share one's most private relationship issues, fears, and needs in front of one's partner, so the therapist must handle each session with incredible care and skill.

This book provides a foundational understanding of the theoretical underpinnings, key concepts, practical interventions, activities, and reference handouts that will allow you to be effective in working with couples. Through a mix of theory, direct learning, and clinical skills, you'll gain broad knowledge on how to understand and treat couples in distress, no matter the presenting problem. You will learn to be a neutral party who supports the relationship—a markedly different approach than for individual therapy—and you should be encouraged to take a stance when it benefits the relationship. To be effective, clinicians working with couples must be empathic while also confronting unproductive beliefs or behaviors that are negatively impacting the relationship. Not only will you gain knowledge and skills to strengthen your work, but you will also be given information on further training, certification paths, books, and additional resources that will help you find a starting place and continue to grow in this specialty.

Chapter 1 introduces important aspects of working with couples, starting with how this form of therapy differs from individual therapy and the additional skills therapists need to develop. You will learn to view and navigate the therapeutic relationship with the couple, including rapport building, managing biases, and staying present—particularly during escalated conflict. The chapter explains why you, as the therapist, need to increase your comfort with conflict, sexually explicit language, and discussions about difficult issues, such as infidelity. Here, you may realize some work you need to do regarding your own countertransference patterns, biases, judgments, anxieties, and discomforts. Finally, this chapter also covers important aspects of assessment, goals and "successes" in couples work, and termination.

Chapter 2 provides background on the main theories and orientations that underlie working with couples. You will explore the most prominent couples therapy approaches, such as cognitive behavioral couples therapy (CBCT), The Gottman Method, emotionally focused therapy (EFT), and Imago relationship therapy, and also look into critical theories on sex therapy. You'll explore both the historical and present research in sex therapy from psychoanalysis to multidisciplinary approaches. In addition, you will learn how (and why) to conduct relationship and sexual functioning assessments that will serve you when working with any presenting concern. In short, this chapter sets the foundation for the pursual of any possible future training or certifications.

Chapter 3 gives an overview of how attachment theory explains both the importance of relationships and the significant impact that relational distress has on individuals. You will learn the attachment styles and how they may present during conflict. From there, the chapter discusses the importance of identifying and working with the negative cycle in relationship conflict, explains how to help clients identify maladaptive learned messages and internalized beliefs about love and relationships, and provides guidance for navigating typical roles and patterns that lead to disconnection. You will gain a greater understanding of how to identify and work with the most common dynamics behind attachment distress.

Chapter 4 focuses on emotional regulation. It explains why regulation is a key relationship skill, describes the biological processes and physiological symptoms of emotional flooding (known colloquially as *fight or flight*), and provides strategies for self-soothing. You will learn that understanding and working with internal and external emotional boundaries can strengthen self-regulation, which will help you identify when a client is emotionally dysregulated and offer guidance in how to support them. Finally, you will learn about how coregulation strengthens relational attachment and why self-regulation is a necessary building block for this ability.

Chapter 5 begins by providing critical information about conflict and the relationship cycle of harmony, rupture, and repair. It explains what beliefs and behaviors trigger or escalate conflicts, how conflict can be self-sustaining due to the negative cycle, and why poor emotional boundaries can make managing conflict even more challenging. Here, you will learn about conflict styles and errors that escalate emotional volatility and disconnection during arguments. The chapter finishes by providing clear and practical guidance on how couples can best manage conflict, from effective communication skills to de-escalation and repair strategies.

Chapter 6 focuses on special topics in couples work. First, it looks at what clinicians should know when working with couples in non-monogamous relationships. Next, it discusses infidelity and other ruptures of trust, providing background on the challenges of working with this issue, the stages of healing, and a roadmap for repair. From there, you will learn the difference between discernment counseling and couples therapy, including the nuanced view and approach that therapists must take in these different situations. Finally, this chapter provides an understanding of abuse in relationships. It defines several types of abuse, explains the cycle of abuse, and teaches you what to do when you suspect or know that abuse is occurring.

Chapter 7 answers the questions *Why is sex important?* and *What is sexual "functioning"?* In this chapter, you will gain insight regarding the functions of sex, the motivations to have sex, and the factors that contribute to sexual experiences. Just as important, you will learn how to identify sex-negative residue and educate your clients on sex positivity, why it's important, and how shifting to a more sex-positive framework can help address their sexual challenges.

Chapter 8 investigates desire and arousal. Not only will you be able to define desire and arousal, but through learning about the dual-control model of arousal, you will be equipped to explain to your clients why they experience (or don't experience) desire and arousal in the ways that they think they should. Furthermore, you will learn about such phenomena as differing sensitivities of inhibitory and excitatory systems, concordant arousal, and discordant arousal. This chapter is where you will learn how to tackle the most prevalent issue in sex therapy: desire discrepancy.

Chapter 9 tackles the most important topic in sex therapy: communicating about intimacy. In addition to learning how to communicate effectively with your vulnerable clients, you will develop the ability to teach them how to communicate with others. This chapter draws on skills learned earlier in the book (emotional regulation, conflict resolution, etc.) and builds upon them with issues related to sexuality, such as shame. Specifically, you will learn models of communication that empower clients to speak openly and honestly about sex and sexuality, and you will get the opportunity to see these models in practice through clinical vignettes.

Chapter 10 introduces some special topics in sex therapy. While many couples approach sex therapy with some form of desire discrepancy, many other issues can challenge the sex lives of your clients. Here, you will learn briefly about various diagnoses related to sexuality, ethical non-monogamy, BDSM and kink, aging, disability, and illness. (Note that while abuse and infidelity are also specific issues in sex therapy, they are covered in chapter 6.)

Chapter 11 addresses how you can continue to build and strengthen your skills in working with couples. It discusses the benefit of individual and group supervision, considerations for pursuing more training or certifications, and recommendations for further reading and additional resources.

Working with couples can feel daunting, even for the seasoned clinician. If you have had challenging experiences working with couples, you are not alone. Do not be discouraged. It takes training, practice, and supervision to master the skills of couples and sex therapy. While it requires unique training and a different approach from individual work, it can be an interesting and exciting addition to your practice—one that encourages you to develop more self-awareness and skills as you support your clients. It's likely that you will also experience insights about yourself and your own romantic relationships. You may discover how your attachment style or unhelpful behaviors are contributing to the negative cycle in your relationship, any unresolved issues or needs that have not been addressed with your partner, or even the latent biases and judgments about relationships or sex that have impacted your relationship or even your clinical work. This is part of the work for any therapist specializing in working with couples. We cannot help others without first knowing ourselves, and this book will hold up a mirror so you can see what you are bringing into the room.

Whether this is the first step on your path to specialization or you have already taken trainings or classes in this work, we are glad you're here and look forward to equipping you with vital knowledge and abilities for working effectively with couples.

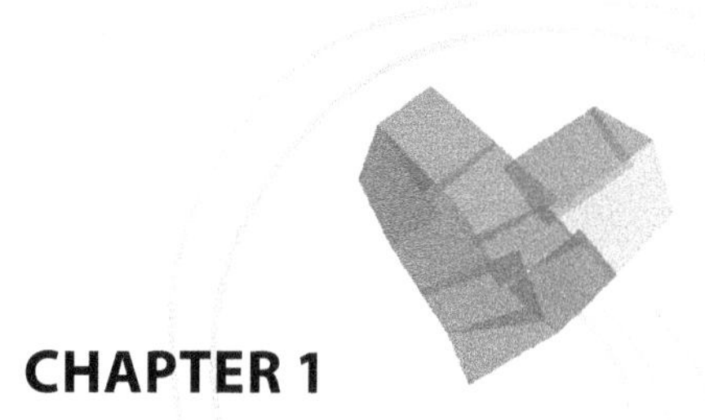

CHAPTER 1

Working with Couples

Welcome to *Navigating Intimacy*, a book that introduces foundational knowledge and teaches key interventions for working with couples. In this chapter, you will learn the basics of couples and sex therapy, including:

- Establishing and maintaining a therapeutic alliance
- Defining success and goals of treatment
- Identifying the necessary parts of an effective assessment
- Understanding contraindications for treatment
- Considering termination

Individual Therapy versus Couples Therapy

Many clinicians approach couples work in the same way they would individual therapy. This is understandable given that most therapists are trained almost exclusively in individual therapy. However, it will not be effective to simply transfer your strategies for individual therapy into couples therapy. When working with couples, you will need to monitor more complicated therapeutic alliances, be attuned to everyone in the room (including yourself), and be more active in sessions.

Perhaps the most important difference in couples therapy is that creating an alliance is more nuanced and challenging, and maintaining rapport requires close attunement and clear communication. There will be times when one client feels you are favoring their partner, and a rupture with one or both clients can have unexpected ripple effects in the room and in their relationship. Although it can feel daunting at first, the key takeaways are that you can address any therapeutic ruptures through attunement, that checking in with your clients is important, and that effective repair is essential. (These principles will be discussed in depth later in this chapter.)

Another critical difference in couples work is that you need to be in charge of the session as opposed to letting clients take the lead. Without a strong therapist leading the work, couples are likely to spend the entire session fighting and reinforcing unhelpful, damaging patterns. The goal of couples work is to help clients gain insight into their emotions and behaviors, share vulnerable feelings, and interrupt negative cycles of communicating. None of that can happen if the therapist sits back. Couples, particularly escalated ones, need to be taught to pause, de-escalate, and learn new ways of interacting. This requires the therapist to be more active and engaged in these sessions compared to individual therapy.

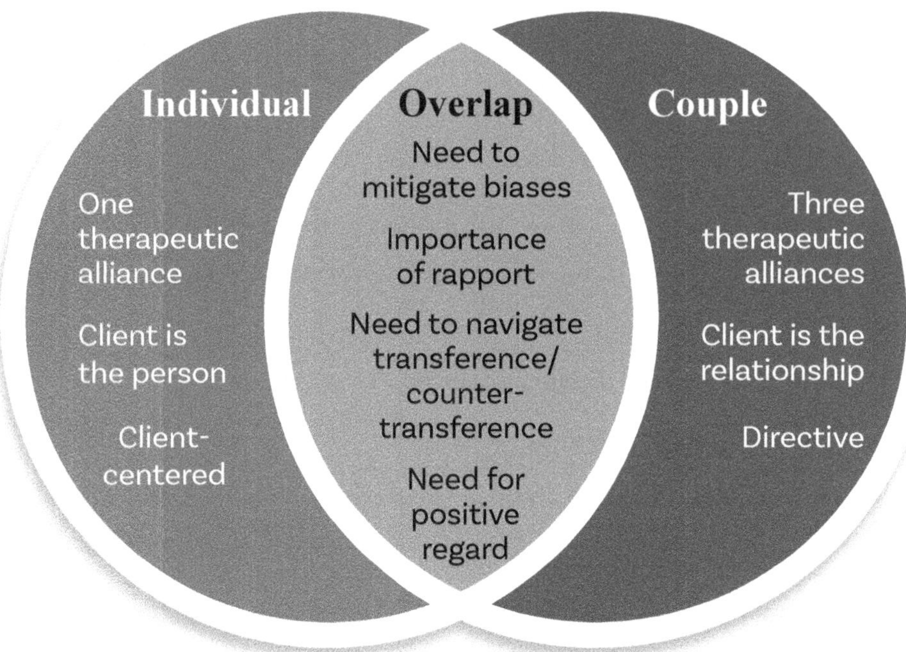

Sex Therapy versus General Psychotherapy

While sex therapy and general psychotherapy share many aspects, there are four important elements that make sex therapy distinct: shame; sex positivity; comfort and confidence; and explicit language.

Shame

When discussing sex and sexuality, your clients will inevitably encounter layers of shame. Lack of adequate sexual education, stigma around what is and is not considered acceptable, and sex-negative cultural messaging combine to create the perfect storm of secrecy and shame. Many of your clients may be speaking about their sexuality for the very first time in your office. It is mandatory that you demonstrate sensitivity to the discomfort that your clients may be experiencing.

Part of the work of sex therapy is breaking down this wall of shame. It is vital to help your clients identify their shame and understand the outside influences that created it and continue to maintain it. Exploring your clients' sources of information about sex and the covert messaging they received around sex is important in this process. Who spoke to them about sex? What did these people say? What did they learn from movies, TV, pornography, rumors, and peer relationships? After identifying and breaking down the sex-negative influences in their personal development, you can work with them to move toward a more sex-positive stance on sex and sexuality.

Sex Positivity

It is of utmost importance that a therapist working with a couple around sexual issues embodies a sex-positive stance. Progress in sex therapy depends on reducing shame and promoting sexual well-being. As the therapist, it is vital that you model this positivity, demonstrating to your clients that there is an alternative to the sex negativity that has surrounded them most of their lives. Demonstrating positive regard and affirmation of your clients' sexualities not only empowers them to openly share their thoughts and feelings around sexuality but also gives them a target to move toward, rather than something to just move away from.

Sex positivity includes the following:

- A positive and nonjudgmental view of sex and sexuality
- The understanding that sex is a positive aspect of life as opposed to a taboo
- Respect and openness to others' sexuality
- Comfort and confidence in one's own sexuality

Sex positivity does not require you to find erotic value in everything that your clients find erotic, but rather to respect that it holds erotic value for them. They will likely experience shame around some aspects of their sexuality, and it is tremendously valuable to model a nonjudgmental, positive attitude toward topics that they may feel conflicted about. In doing so, you provide your clients with an alternate way of relating to such aspects of their sexuality. You give them the opportunity, whether they take it or not, to understand their sexuality in a non-shameful and potentially positive light. In essence, through your sex-positive stance, you are teaching your clients how to find sex positivity in their own lives.

Comfort and Confidence

The need for comfort and confidence is paramount in sex therapy. You are dealing with very sensitive subject matter, and your clients are looking to you for comfort and hope. It is imperative that you are confident in what you know as well as what you don't know. It is not required that you be an expert in all things sexual; rather, you must be an expert in the limits of your own comfort and confidence. Remember, comfort and confidence can be gained with additional exploration, training, and supervision. If you're not there yet, you can always refer clients out if a case is beyond the scope of what you can offer.

Explicit Language

Finally, it is extremely important within sex therapy to use explicit language with shared definitions. For example, many people use the term *sex* to describe penile-vaginal intercourse exclusively. However, sex actually encompasses any behavior that holds erotic value to a person. Thus, it is necessary to know what your clients actually mean when they say that they are dissatisfied with sex. Similarly, explicit language is required for its specificity. While it does not necessarily matter whether your clients use the word *teste* or *ball*, you want to make sure that everyone in the session is clear on what this word in particular means. Make sure that you check with your clients about the language they use to create explicit language with shared definitions. Additionally, it's worth observing whether you have felt uncomfortable reading some of the terms in this book so far. If these terms, or others that you can think of, make you feel awkward or self-conscious, practice saying them in front of the mirror until they become second nature.

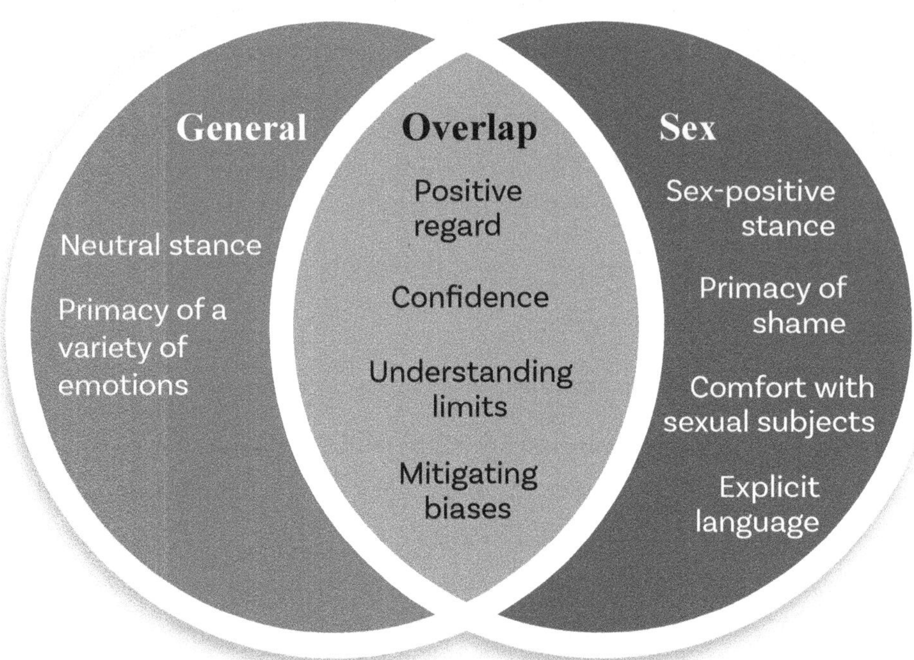

Establishing and Maintaining the Therapeutic Relationship

Just as with all therapy, a good therapeutic alliance is crucial for couples work. A strong alliance means that the therapist and clients are mutually invested in the work, share a collaborative attitude, and work together toward shared goals (Pinsof & Catherall, 1986). For couples, this requires the therapist to establish safety, connect emotionally with all clients, and ensure both partners are participating in the creation and pursuit of shared goals (Friedlander et al., 2008). Since the strength of the therapeutic rapport can predict progress, focusing on the alliance early on in treatment is essential (Friedlander et al., 2008; Tilden et al., 2021). An important reframe you'll need to make when working with couples is that instead of an individual being the client, *the relationship is your client.*

While holding the relationship as your client, you must also maintain an empathic, nonjudgmental stance with *all* partners. In other words, you are empathizing with and advocating for everyone in the room as you try to help the relationship. Maintaining a strong rapport with everyone is no simple matter when you consider not just the many alliances in the room, but the many perceptions of alliances. You have to be aware of your alliance with each partner, the alliance between you and your clients as a couple, *and* your clients' perceptions of your alliance with their partner. For partnerships with more than two individuals, the alliances and perceptions of alliances obviously increase in number and complexity.

Tracking these alliances can be challenging. For instance, the following graphic shows all the different alliances at work when seeing a two-person couple.

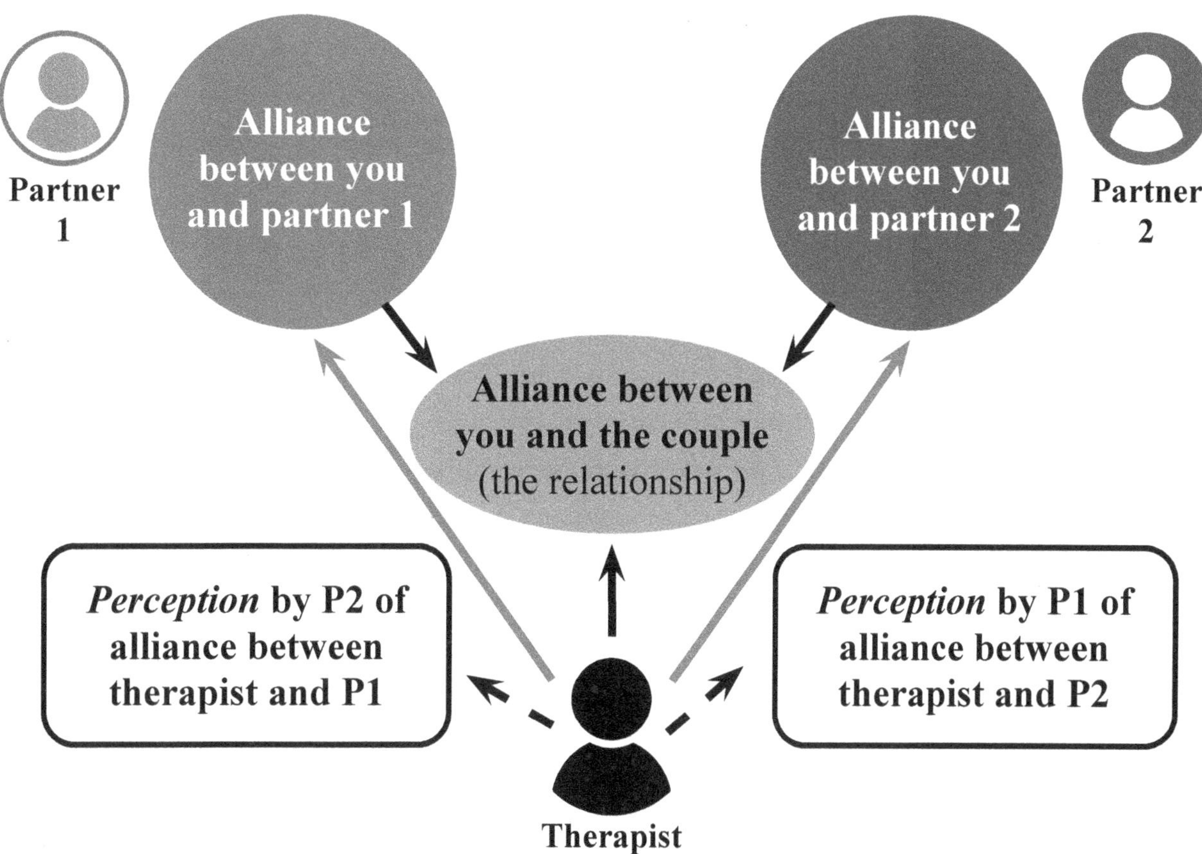

Many therapists also practice virtually now, and it's important to note that these alliances—and the outcomes of couples therapy—are no different with virtual sessions. However, some research shows it may take longer to establish rapport in virtual therapy compared to in-person couples work (Bradford et al., 2024).

Many couples enter therapy fearful that the therapist will take the other person's side. Clients need to know that they will be heard and supported by you, so being explicit about your approach during the consultation or first session is a helpful approach. For example, you might say:

> "Unlike with individual therapy, I'm not here to be entirely on one person's side. I'm here to support your relationship, and my goal will be to help both of you make positive changes so that you can have the happiest relationship possible."

As with individual work, the best strategy for establishing rapport is to fully understand and accept each partner's experience. However, being empathic and nonjudgmental does not mean always being neutral. As you'll read later in this book, it's imperative that therapists identify key points of change by holding clients accountable for their actions and challenging unhelpful or destructive beliefs while maintaining a warm regard. You may end up temporarily "siding" with one partner if doing so leads to important insight and change for the relationship. However, you must be able to rebalance the alliance with all clients.

Establishing rapport and managing alliances are equally important when discussing sex with couples. In fact, the therapeutic relationship in sex therapy with couples is markedly similar to that of general psychotherapy with couples, though there are some notable additions. For example, when discussing issues of sex and sexuality, the therapist must be acutely cognizant of their framing of the sexual issue, their stance toward sexuality, their own boundaries, and the importance of centering consent.

Careful Framing of the Sexual Issue

Many couples come to sex therapy with an idea of "who" the problem lies with. You must reframe that problem as external to the couple, and the individual partners will act as a team working against the problem. For example, one topic you will inevitably encounter in sex therapy is *desire discrepancy*, which is a difference in preferences around the quantity, quality, or type of sex that each partner desires. This will occur between partners in almost every sexual relationship simply because a relationship consists of two (or more) separate identities. To address the desires of each partner with appropriate care and respect, you must work to reframe the issue as resulting from the combination of each partners' preferences as opposed to the result of any one partner's preferences. By reframing the nature of the problem, you reduce the potential for a power struggle, shame, or a blaming situation.

Stance Toward Sexuality

While sex positivity is a central tenet of sex therapy, it is important to understand that you will be challenged to maintain this stance with every aspect of sexuality that you encounter. Even as you acquire additional training, supervision, and consultation on more challenging aspects of sexuality, you will inevitably find yourself having difficulty with certain topics. These topics represent your limitations as a sex therapist. While it is your duty to expand your beliefs and attitudes, it is also important to know and respect your limitations. There is danger in taking on aspects of sexuality that you are uncomfortable or upset by—to do this risks further shame and damage toward your clients. Every therapist has some limitations, and it is therefore essential that you are aware of yours so you can refer these clients out.

Boundaries

In addition to being cognizant of your own boundaries, you must also take care to recognize boundary crossings in the therapeutic environment. As you can imagine, the content of sex therapy sessions is likely to be sexual in nature. However, it is your responsibility to make a distinction between sexual content versus *sexualized* content. Sexual content simply involves speaking about sexual issues or topics. Sexualized content, on the other hand, involves discussing such topics with the (possibly unconscious) intention of exciting or objectifying the other person. Similarly, it is important to make a distinction between erotic and *eroticized* transference. Due to the intimate nature of therapy, it is likely and perhaps helpful for positive feelings to develop toward the therapist—this is known as *erotic transference*. Eroticized transference, on the other hand, involves unconscious desires to love, have sex with, or possess the therapist. These are complex topics that are beyond the scope of this book; therapists doing this type of work should pursue further education (see chapter 11 for recommended resources).

Should you identify that sexualized content or eroticized transference may be at play, it is always a good idea to seek supervision. Ultimately, this behavior should be confronted and used to deepen the client's understanding of what is happening and reestablish safer boundaries in treatment.

Centering Consent

Consent is central to good sex and good sex therapy. It is important that you model for your clients how to ask for consent when broaching sensitive topics or suggesting behavioral interventions. By asking for consent, you are empowering your clients to set the boundaries that they need to feel comfortable and open with you. Furthermore, by centering consent in the treatment, you lay the foundation for your clients to develop the vital skill of asking for consent with one another in moments of vulnerability and intimacy.

Defining Success in Couples Therapy

Couples often feel hopeless and lost by the time they make it to therapy. They may explain their distress in words like:

- "We have the same fights over and over about the smallest things. We just don't communicate well."
- "We've had the same sexual problems for years, but we can't seem to figure it out."
- "We love each other and have an amazing family, but we're so disconnected from each other. We avoid talking about hard things because it never goes well."
- "My partner doesn't want to have sex with me."

- "My partner wants to have sex all the time."
- "We both feel unheard, like the other person isn't listening or doesn't get how we feel. And we feel worse after talking instead of better."
- "Everything else in our relationship is great—we just have some trouble when it comes to sex."
- "It feels like we're walking on eggshells with each other because everything turns into an argument."
- "We're in a rut. Our sex life is routine, and we don't know how to spice things up."

After years of desperately wanting to change their relationship but not knowing how, and perhaps multiple failed attempts to fix their problems on their own, people tend to come into the treatment session with lofty goals. They may even aim for a completely conflict-free, emotionally and sexually intimate, easy, enjoyable relationship, wanting to continue therapy to optimize their interactions past the point of usefulness. Though therapists would love to provide all couples with this ultimate goal, it's important to set realistic expectations. For example, while there is no such thing as a conflict-free relationship, there are relationships where conflict is managed effectively and leads to greater connection. Similarly, no sexual relationship can deliver spontaneous, earth-shatteringly lustful intimacy on every occasion, but there are relationships in which deeply fulfilling sexual intimacy is consistently achieved through communication and compassion.

You can help couples set the right expectations and goals by normalizing the challenges that even happy, healthy relationships experience. According to research by the Gottman Institute, 69 percent of all relationship conflicts are perpetual and unresolvable, meaning that couples will have the same fights for their entire relationship (Gottman & Gottman, 2008). This is not meant to scare them, but to show them that getting rid of conflict isn't the mark of relational success. Instead, success in couples therapy is equipping each partner with the skills to communicate, de-escalate, and repair. The ultimate goal should be the ability to effectively navigate conflict when it arises.

Additionally, some clients may hope you will fundamentally change their partner in ways that are not possible (nor recommended). For instance, they may think you can convince their partner to stop being messy or to be more punctual. These specific behavioral changes are not the real problem; the issue underlying these gripes is how the clients *feel* when their partners are messy or late. Couples will try to focus on the content of their fights; your job is to help them dig deeper to resolve the real problem lingering beneath the content.

Success can also include the ending of a relationship. Although this is usually not the goal of working with couples, helping clients realize that the relationship is not healthy or not serving them can be a positive outcome. Particularly in the case of abusive relationships, helping clients see that their dynamic is abusive can free them from an unhealthy relationship.

Even in relationships that don't involve abuse, there are many circumstances when a couple may be better off separating instead of staying together. For example, if there are truly incompatible needs or goals that they cannot reconcile, such as only one partner wanting children or partners' sexual needs being mutually exclusive, a couple may benefit from parting ways. Another example may be a couple where one partner does not have much affection or empathy left for the other after years of conflict and disconnection. Therapy may help this couple see that they no longer have a foundation, and it may be better to let each other go.

When an ICU doctor is treating a wounded patient, the doctor can do everything "right" but still be unable to save the patient. Sometimes this happens in couples work as well. A therapist can help partners communicate better, understand each other more, and foster intimacy and closeness, but it's up to the clients to determine if there is mutual commitment and desire to continue the relationship. If you see couples who decide to end their relationship, this is not a "failure." If you help your clients communicate their feelings and needs and this results in a realization that they no longer want to be together, that is a successful outcome. That said, deciding to end a relationship is not something that you can recommend (outside of clearly abusive relationships where therapy is contraindicated—more on that later in this chapter).

Defining success is of paramount importance with regard to sex therapy in particular. When clients enter treatment, they often have expectations around what their sex life should involve, what they think other people's sex lives involve, or what unattainable ideal they are in pursuit of. Expectations such as these must be tempered with the reality that a perfect sex life, whatever that may mean, does not exist. Instead, we must aim for "good enough sex" (McCarthy & Metz, 2012) and "optimal sex" (Kleinplatz et al., 2009).

The Good Enough Sex (GES) model is a sex-positive, multifaceted model that promotes "realistically vibrant and relationship-sustaining sex that serves a number of values and purposes—pleasure, affirmation, tension release, couple cohesion, self-esteem, lust, emotional intimacy, excitement, comfort, and/or reproduction" (McCarthy & Metz, 2012, p. 214). In the GES model, the role of the therapist is to help couples adopt and work toward a uniquely defined "good enough" sex life. Similarly, Kleinplatz and colleagues (2009) proposed the concept of *optimal*, rather than ideal, sex. This model identified nine major components of optimal sex, including being present, connecting, mutual respect, caring and acceptance, communication, interpersonal risk taking, authenticity, vulnerability, and a sense of transcendence. Both the GES and optimal sex models focus on the complexities of sexual experience rather than reductionist views focused on function versus dysfunction or normal versus abnormal. When working with your clients around sexual issues, it is essential to manage their expectations and promote the GES and optimal models to help construct realistic, sex-positive definitions of success.

Repairing from Ruptures

Couples therapists need to become skilled at checking in with clients, particularly after possible ruptures. Ruptures are inevitable; moreover, they aren't always an indication that you did something wrong.

Nevertheless, it's vital to consider how you will respond when they occur. Ruptures can be detrimental to the work if not handled correctly, but responding with curiosity and a desire to repair can lead to significant change. Rather than exhibit unhelpful behaviors in response to a rupture, such as defensiveness, dismissiveness, or denial, you can demonstrate a healthy response by taking responsibility and showing curiosity and care. This alone can be healing for the client, who may not have had anyone in their life show them such empathy. It's equally as important for their partner to witness, as it provides a roadmap for how they can manage ruptures in their relationship outside of session.

There are many kinds of ruptures you may encounter. These can be distilled into two categories: *withdrawal ruptures* and *confrontation ruptures* (Safran & Muran, 2006). Confrontation ruptures are usually easy to detect—they occur when a client openly disagrees with something you say or expresses negativity toward you. Withdrawal ruptures can be harder to spot, since it may look like your client is quietly listening and participating when, in fact, they are hurt, leading them to avoid engagement and resist interventions.

It can be challenging to determine how clients are feeling with so much happening in the room. Directly asking clients about their emotional state is the best way to understand what they are feeling and assess the state of your alliance with them. For instance, if you suspect you have upset a client, an appropriate approach would be to directly ask if something you said has upset them, use clarifying questions to ensure you understand why your words impacted them, and empathically validate their feelings. Bring the focus to the present moment, to what happened that hurt the client, and explore that experience with them. As you do so, acknowledge your part in the rupture and take responsibility for it. You should reinforce how glad you are that they are sharing their feelings and processing this rupture with you—this will promote a sense of emotional safety and encourage them (or their partner) to speak up if future ruptures occur.

It's important to also check in with their partner who observed the rupture to understand their experience of what happened and offer them an opportunity to be supportive and empathic of their partner (Swank & Wittenborn, 2013). Remember, not only is this good practice for you to reestablish rapport, but it is also beneficial for the partner to observe you modeling how to be curious and empathic following a rupture. In doing this, you are not only teaching but showing both partners how to address problems; perhaps more importantly, they can see that it works.

Ruptures can make some therapists anxious or insecure. Some may fear that they are not doing a good job if they upset a client. However, making errors and hurting clients is inevitable in this work; it occurs frequently even for the most skilled clinicians (Safran & Muran, 1996). There are many competing needs and feelings in the room, and even expressing understanding and validation to one partner could upset the other if they are in a particularly sensitive emotional space. You need to be comfortable with ruptures because avoiding them entirely is simply not possible. Just as in an intimate partnership, ruptures between you and your clients can truly be a benefit to the work if you handle them correctly. The goal is never to be perfect, but rather to handle mistakes effectively. The following therapist reference handout includes the essential information you will need to manage and repair a rupture.

Therapist Reference

Repairing from Ruptures

Ruptures in couples work are inevitable, just like conflicts in romantic relationships. Instead of fearing them, you can use them as opportunities to strengthen rapport with your clients while modeling how they can address ruptures in their own relationship. The following strategies can help you directly address a rupture with a client in session:

- **Identify the rupture:** Being attuned to your client will allow you to notice when a rupture has occurred. Observe if their emotional states suddenly change or if you feel a disconnection from them. Remember to look for both confrontation and withdrawal ruptures, which present quite differently. Consider how what you said or did might have triggered this response.
- **Acknowledge and be curious about the rupture:** Directly ask your client if something you said has upset them, use clarifying questions to ensure you understand why your words impacted them, and empathically validate their feelings.
- **Do not respond in a way that will make the client feel worse:** This includes defensiveness, dismissiveness, or denial. By challenging, minimizing, or ignoring the rupture, you show a lack of empathy and communicate the idea that your client's feelings don't matter to you. This will damage your relationship with the client, and it's possible to damage the rapport with the couple as a whole if their partner also dislikes how you have responded to the rupture.
- **Repair from the rupture:** Name and acknowledge that a rupture happened. Bring attention to the present moment in session and be curious about what you said or did that hurt the client. Ask your client to share their feelings with you; be curious, attentive, and empathic as they do. Take responsibility for your part in the rupture and apologize. Be sure to reinforce your client as they take the risk of sharing what happened and what they are feeling. Finally, check in with the other partner to see how they experienced the rupture and do similar repair with them as needed.
- **Model and provide psychoeducation on repair:** As you and your client address and heal from the rupture, you can point out this as an example of relationship repair. Talk through the process: realize the rupture, explore it with curiosity, express empathy and remorse, and reconnect.

Navigating Biases

No therapist is a "clean slate." Since you're human, it's inevitable that you will be biased or feel pulled more toward one client at times. These biases may come from a variety of sources. For example, a shared life experience may make it easier for you to maintain rapport with one partner more than the other. If you've been cheated on by someone you loved, you might find it challenging to work with couples who are healing from infidelity. Other biases may come from your personal preferences or beliefs. Hearing someone speaking harshly may make you feel protective of their partner, or your definition of a "good relationship" may lead you to unnecessarily question a couple who have found an arrangement that works for them.

It is normal to have these small shifts in empathy and alliance, but you must be aware of and manage them so they don't impact the work. If you are unaware of your underlying beliefs and biases, you may inadvertently steer a relationship in the wrong direction for the given couple.

This makes it essential to increase your self-awareness of what you might find difficult or where you feel more natural empathy.

With regard to sex therapy, however, you should always maintain a bias toward sex positivity. Rather than remaining neutral, avoiding bias in sex therapy has more to do with overcoming your own sex negativity and shame in order to promote positivity and well-being for your clients. For example, many of us are brought up in a culture that promotes monogamy. However, many people are not monogamous, and their well-being is better supported in an ethically non-monogamous (ENM) relationship structure. It is not enough to tolerate an ENM structure; it is imperative that you understand how a culture of monogamy has taught you sometimes unhelpful and untrue beliefs around sexual exclusivity so that you may be affirming of ENM relationship structures.

Use the following therapist reflection to examine some of the common biases that come up when working with conflict and sex in couples therapy.

Therapist Reflection

Identifying Biases

Our personal identity and experiences can often result in blind spots when it comes to how we view others' relationships. These blind spots are typically the root causes of our unconscious assumptions and biases. Take the time to explore your own biases; knowing this information about yourself will help you advise couples in the right direction for their specific relationship.

Ask yourself:

Do you think any degree of yelling, stonewalling, or blaming is unacceptable?

____

____

____

Do you see one partner's repeated requests for more help around the house as "nagging?" Alternatively, do you see the other partner as being lazy?

____

____

____

Do you believe that having kids means a couple should stay together no matter what?

____

____

____

Do you think relationships can recover from infidelity? What about recurring infidelity with different extramarital partners? An affair that lasted months or years?

____

____

____

When treating a couple where one partner wants more sex, do you tend to agree that the partner with lower desire should try to increase the frequency of sexual intimacy?

____

____

____

What observations or experiences in your life may have led to certain beliefs or biases that could influence how you view your clients and their relationship? (Consider your parents' relationship, your own prior romantic relationships, and other factors that may play a role in your perspective.)

____

____

____

Now, consider the following list of treatment scenarios. What images, adjectives, and thoughts first come to mind when you imagine these relationships?

Couples of differing:

Races

____

____

Religions

____

____

Ages

____

____

Sexual orientations

____

____

Socioeconomic statuses

Couples with a history of:

Substance use

Chronic infidelity

Emotional abuse

Relationship structures, including:

Polyamory

Ethical non-monogamy

Committed but unmarried

Noncommitted

Dyadic monogamy

Sexual interests, including:

Fetishes

Kinks

BDSM

Historically de-sexualized individuals, including:

The elderly

Overweight people

People with physical disabilities

People with cognitive disabilities

Now, answer the following questions based on your personal beliefs.

What are the goals of a relationship?

____

____

____

____

____

What is a healthy amount or kind of sex?

____

____

____

____

____

What does a good relationship look like?

____

____

____

____

____

The answers to the prompts and questions that you have provided are the biases that you bring into the therapy room with you. Take care to pursue education and supervision to address those that would prohibit you from promoting your clients' ideas of what relationship and sexual fulfillment are to them. It is everyone's right to pursue a relationship and sexual well-being as they define it. It is your job to support their pursuit by identifying, understanding, and managing your own biases.

Managing Intense Affect

Not only do you need to be aware of your clients' emotional states and your alliance with each partner, but you also need to be aware of how *you* are feeling in the room. Working with couples can be more emotionally volatile than individual therapy and can include sexually explicit content, both of which can be challenging (or even dysregulating) for therapists. Imagine the worst fight that you've had with a partner, then imagine being a third person witnessing that fight and whose job it is to actively intervene and take charge of the situation. That can feel scary, and understandably so. The following pages will provide you with the tools needed to manage these harder moments in session.

Remember that *you* are steering the ship. The couple is seeking help precisely because they have been unable to navigate these conversations and conflicts on their own. You have to take the lead, especially during escalated moments. Your role can be summed up into three Cs—contain, calm, and invite curiosity:

- **Contain:** Take control of the moment of conflict. Don't allow the conversation to spiral or clients to escalate. You need to be in charge. Pause the clients, acknowledge that they're caught in their negative cycle, and explain that you're going to help them understand what's happening in this moment.
- **Calm:** Before the clients can process what's happening between them, they need to regulate their nervous systems. Start by validating their feelings so they feel heard and understood. Guide them in taking a few deep breaths or try another strategy for helping them self-soothe. They can take a five-minute break to walk or get some water; whatever it takes to calm themselves down.
- **Curiosity:** Once your clients are regulated, invite them to be curious about what occurred that led to the escalation. This is an opportunity to identify triggers that lead to strong emotional reactions as well as the painful feelings that fuel their outward reactions. When a person is upset, what they want most is for their partner to be patient, empathic, and curious; you can model that in session for the couple.

This approach to in-session conflict management is simple enough, but it can be very challenging to pause clients when they are escalated. They will try to continue the fight, often having "one last thing to say" that will continue or worsen the argument. Many couples resist being stopped—that is normal. In fact, it's exactly why they came to therapy. Their way of fighting has become ingrained, and learning a new way will require you to take charge and lead by example.

Just as you'll be supporting your clients in strengthening their emotion regulation and self-soothing skills, you'll need to do the same for yourself. Watching a couple fight can be upsetting, and you will need to have strategies to keep yourself calm and grounded. You may need to do a deep breathing exercise or even stop the couple's argument and lead everyone in a few deep breaths. Preparing for emotional stress before the session is also helpful, such as doing a deep breathing practice, exercising, spending time in nature or with a pet, reading, meditating, or another calming activity. Doing similar self-care tasks after difficult sessions will help as well. You can also use the following therapist reflection to develop your own self-soothing plan for when you feel dysregulated. You need to be attuned to your body and be aware of your emotional state. These strategies will not help if you don't realize how upset you are.

Finally, it's important to be aware of your triggers, biases, and personal and professional limits—and know it's acceptable to be selective. This knowledge will help you anticipate the harder moments, but you can also choose not to work with certain couples at any time if you find their presenting problem or argument style too dysregulating to provide effective therapy. Identifying those couples prior to working together can be a challenge; this will be addressed in our next discussion on assessment.

Therapist Reflection

Developing a Self-Soothing Plan

All therapists must identify their limits, regardless of what population they choose to treat. Take a moment to imagine how you will feel when working with an angry, escalated couple (or perhaps think back to a session when this happened) and reflect on the following questions.

How do you know when you are emotionally escalated and need to engage in self-soothing?

____

____

____

What self-soothing tools will you use before, during, and after sessions?

____

____

____

Will working with escalated couples be too dysregulating for you? How will you ensure difficult sessions do not significantly impact the rest of your day or even week?

____

____

____

Are there any forms of communication that you know you'll struggle to be effective with (e.g., couples who scream or swear, couples who are silent when angry, couples that sling personal insults)?

____

____

____

What will you do if a couple doesn't listen when you try to interrupt and de-escalate them?

What self-soothing techniques will you use with couples during sessions to help them regulate their emotions? Will you feel comfortable leading them in these strategies?

Therapist Reference

Pausing and De-escalating Couples in Session

It's important that you are in charge of the session. When your clients are in an escalated emotional state, you need to intervene. The following strategies can help you directly intervene when clients escalate:

- Use a strong, assertive voice to interrupt your clients.
- If they do not stop, you can use hand gestures (such as making a "T" and saying, "Wait a minute—time out") or wave your hands in front of you.
- For couples who are very escalated and angry, you can flip the lights in the room to get their attention. (If you're practicing virtually, you can turn off your camera to catch their attention.)
- Explain that you stopped them because they are caught in their negative cycle and the argument will only worsen if it continues. Tell them they're here so that you can help them get *out* of these moments and find a better way to communicate.
- Check in with each of them; find out how they're feeling. Help them self-soothe and calm their nervous systems as needed.
- Prompt them to be curious about how the conversation escalated into conflict. Without assigning blame, look at what words or nonverbal cues caused a reaction in the other person.
- Present this as an opportunity to see how conflicts escalate, and more importantly, an opportunity to better understand each other.

General Assessment for Couples

Couples work should start with an in-depth assessment. This accomplishes two things: it establishes rapport with each client by getting to know them, and it looks for contraindications to therapy. The challenge is that couples already know the information you're asking and will be eager to start working on their relationship instead of spending time providing background information.

Many therapists find that it's helpful to do a comprehensive written intake in addition to the usual in-session assessment. You'll need to gather a lot of information about two or more people in a short amount of time, and the quicker you can get this background, the better. Given that many couples come into therapy in crisis and want to get to work as soon as possible, providing them with a written assessment in their intake paperwork will help you get important information without spending precious session time asking questions that could be answered by checking off a box. Additionally, having this information prior to your session means being better equipped to help and to ask relevant follow-up questions that could impact the work. For example, if a client indicated they struggle to limit their alcohol intake, you can do a further assessment in session to see if they need support with substance use.

Most modalities of couples therapy recommend doing an initial joint session with all partners and then doing individual sessions with each client to gather additional information before joining back together to work on the relationship This is helpful for clients who may not feel comfortable sharing certain information in the group setting. However, this strategy is not mandatory, and some therapists find that they can establish rapport and complete a full assessment without individual meetings. If you choose to hold individual sessions early on, you need to be clear on confidentiality and secrets (more on this in the next section). It's generally recommended to always have an equal number of individual sessions with each client so that you have the chance to maintain the same rapport with everyone—in other words, if you meet individually with one client, you would then meet individually with all other partners.

Informed Consent

Working with couples requires informed consent from the onset of therapy, meaning that the couple is educated about the risks, benefits, and goals of treatment. Informed consent explains important aspects of therapy, ensuring clients voluntarily agree to participate in the therapy only after knowing what to expect. It includes an explanation of the course of treatment, possible risks of engaging in the therapy, intended benefits, the therapist's credentials, the clients' right to withdraw from treatment at any time, any information about fees or payments, and confidentiality.

Giving your clients this information empowers them, promotes their autonomy, and can even strengthen the therapeutic relationship (Snyder & Barnett, 2006). Informed consent is especially important when working with couples since you have multiple people agreeing to a therapy that has risks (i.e., fights could occur or the relationship could end). You should ensure you have a comprehensive written informed consent that all clients sign prior to meeting, and then you should verbally review the most important aspects of the informed consent during your first session.

Informed consent should also include a disclosure of how you will handle client secrets. There are a few approaches to doing so, and you should be clear from the beginning about which one you use (Bass & Quimby, 2006). The four general approaches are as follows: you can keep no secrets, you can share secrets with a client's written consent, you can explain the types of secrets you will disclose, or you can use your professional discretion to decide if confidentiality of any given secret should be maintained (Kuo, 2009). These strategies vary in terms of how much they emphasize honesty and openness in the work, how easy or challenging they make it for clients to feel safe sharing sensitive information that might be critical for you to know, and what your role will be in deciding the limits of confidentiality. When you decide which approach to take, consider that you want to balance maintaining a strong therapeutic rapport with your clients, allowing them to feel safe sharing with you while not concealing information that could undermine or prevent the couple's progress.

In general, it is important to practice informed consent with your conversations, particularly those with sensitive or difficult content. Part of good communication around relationship and sexual issues involves asking permission to discuss them before diving into a challenging topic. Model this behavior by asking your clients if you can discuss an issue before asking about it directly. This gives them the opportunity to assess whether or not they have the emotional bandwidth to delve deeply, and it is important that you respect a "no" as much as you respect a "yes." Remember, even if your clients aren't ready to talk about this issue, you can help prepare them for future conversations around the topic by addressing their discomfort first.

Gathering Key Information

During your consultation and intake, you will want to gather a few key pieces of information. First, you need to know the presenting problem and how each partner experiences it. Sometimes couples will see the problem in the same way, but others will disagree on what the issue is, and you'll need to learn how each person is experiencing distress in the relationship. This will include getting at least an initial understanding of their negative cycle (i.e., the emotional and behavioral patterns of their fights).

Second, you need to assess for contraindications to therapy (more on this later). There are certain situations where couples therapy is not recommended, and you'll need to ensure you are working with couples who are a good fit for treatment. This doesn't mean couples have to be in their best physical and psychological shape to work with you, but you also need to ensure your clients are capable of meaningfully participating in treatment and getting additional support if needed.

Third, gathering a relationship history will help you better understand each client's attachment style, relational sensitivities, interpersonal strengths, and growing edges. As you ask questions about their relationship with their parents (e.g., how parents expressed anger, how conflicts were managed and resolved) and prior romantic relationships (e.g., quality, level of conflict, how they ended), you'll get a sense of each person and what may be contributing to problems in their current relationship. You will also be building rapport with them as you show genuine interest in knowing about their meaningful relationships and how those relationships have impacted them.

Sex-Specific Assessments

Just as in general psychotherapy, a good history and assessment of sexual well-being can appropriately guide a treatment. There are several models of assessment, including the medical model, the PLISSIT model, and the biopsychosocial model.

The Medical Model

The medical model, criticized for its narrow scope and focus on functioning, is a brief assessment of the current presenting issue. This model answers the following questions:

- What is distressing you?
- For how long has this been happening? Has it been lifelong or acquired?
- Has it changed over time?
- Is it situational or generalized?
- What have you tried? Has it been helpful or unhelpful?

A helpful way to remember how to perform such an assessment is the acronym DOUPE.

- **Description** of the problem
- **Onset** (lifelong/acquired, situation/universal, changes over time)
- **Understanding of the problem** from the client's perspective
- **Prior treatment**
- **Expectations**—setting realistic expectations for treatment

While the medical model gathers essential information, it falls short of addressing several issues, including consent and other matters that are outside of the scope of a medical setting. Consent, which will be discussed at length later, is of primary importance when discussing issues of sex and sexuality, be it between you and your clients or between the clients themselves. Modeling consent from the outset of treatment is a crucial aspect of sex therapy.

The PLISSIT Model

To address some of these shortcomings of the medical model, Annon (1976) developed the PLISSIT model.

- **Permission:** Get consent from your client to discuss their sex life.

- **Limited Information:** Elicit limited information about the specific challenges facing your client.
- **Specific Suggestions:** Provide specified recommendations for treatment.
- **Intensive Therapy:** For issues outside of the scope of a brief medical interaction, refer out for therapy.

Biopsychosocial Model

Both the DOUPE and PLISSIT models are helpful for a brief assessment. However, in a therapeutic setting, you have more time and ability to gather comprehensive information according to the biopsychosocial model of sexual well-being. This model examines three major categories, or spheres, of influence on sexual well-being. First, the biological sphere contains a client's medical history, including an assessment of illnesses, medications, and hormonal functioning. The psychological sphere encompasses their psychological well-being, external stressors, subjective sexual experiences, and their cognitions and beliefs around sex. Third, the social sphere includes family beliefs, social and cultural beliefs, and the partner relationship. Taken together, an assessment of these three categories will provide insight into the scope of the issues that your clients face.

Therapist Reference

Sexual Assessment

General Questions

- What is distressing you?
- For how long has this been happening? Has it been lifelong or acquired?
- Has it changed over time?
- Is it situational or generalized?
- What have you tried? Has it been helpful or unhelpful?

DOUPE Model

- **Description** of the problem
- **Onset** (lifelong/acquired, situation/universal, changes over time)
- **Understanding** of the problem from the client's perspective
- **Prior** treatment
- **Expectations**—setting realistic expectations for treatment

PLISSIT Model

- **Permission:** Get consent from your client to discuss their sex life.
- **Limited Information:** Elicit limited information about the specific challenges facing your client.
- **Specific Suggestions:** Provide specified recommendations for treatment.
- **Intensive Therapy:** For issues outside of the scope of a brief medical interaction, refer out for therapy.

Biopsychosocial Model

- **Bio:** Medical history, including an assessment of illnesses, medications, and hormonal functioning

- **Psycho:** Psychological well-being, external stressors, subjective sexual experiences, and cognitions and beliefs around sex
- **Social:** Family beliefs, social and cultural beliefs, and the partner relationship

Contraindications to Couples Therapy

There are several indicators that a couple may not be ready for joint work. In some cases, couples are eager to improve their relationship, but a key part of doing so requires individual work before each person can be an effective partner. In other cases, not all partners are truly invested in the relationship or in doing the work necessary to improve things. The following are the main contraindications for couples work.

Risk of Violence or Abuse

Couples therapy cannot and should not be pursued if the relationship is unsafe.* This means that if there is any domestic violence or indications of the cycle of abuse, you should not pursue couples work and should instead refer these clients to individual therapy, particularly the client who's at risk of the abuse—meaning they are physically, emotionally, or sexually unsafe in the relationship because their partner is engaging in abusive tactics to gain power and control. Attempting to work with a couple in an abusive relationship can do significant harm. This topic is explored in much greater detail in chapter 6.

A brief definition of abuse will help you know how to observe it between partners. Physical abuse is any aggressive or violent behaviors used to control someone. This can include throwing items, slamming doors, punching walls, or physically assaulting the other person. Emotional abuse involves psychological manipulation intended to gain control and power in the relationship. Common tactics by abusers include gaslighting, demeaning, humiliating, mocking their partner in public or private, blaming their partner for everything, isolating their partner from others, controlling their partner's decisions or actions, denying the abuse, and using guilt or threats to control their partner. Sexual abuse includes any sexual act that occurs without consent. This includes sexual acts that occur when consent is coerced or given under duress. Sexual abuse can be verbal (e.g., making suggestive comments or lewd jokes), physical, or emotional (e.g., making someone feel guilty, coercion, threatening violence or punishment). Just as with other forms of abuse, it can be incredibly difficult to determine whether or not sexual abuse may be present.

An abusive relationship is not one that should be saved. Keeping people in an abusive situation is damaging for everyone involved. The at-risk partner needs individual support, and the perpetrating partner needs help managing their anger, recognizing their abusive behaviors, and taking responsibility. Some partners will be able to do this work and some will not. It's not your job, nor is it possible, to help every abusive partner see the error in their ways and change. Additionally, trying to work with these couples can put the victim in harm's way. Asking a victim to advocate for themselves could enrage their partner and lead to more abuse outside of session. A premature termination by the couple is also likely, leaving the at-risk partner in an even more unsupported and precarious position in the relationship. While you may feel drawn to help this couple out of their toxic situation, you need to remember that doing so can actually cause more harm.

---

* If a client is not safe in their relationship, you can give them the number and website to the National Domestic Violence Hotline: 1-800-799-7233, thehotline.org

Assessing for abuse in a relationship can be challenging and may take a few sessions. If couples aren't aware that their experience qualifies as abuse, or if they aren't forthright about disclosing abusive behaviors such as physical violence, you may not know it is happening at first. Further, the cycle of abuse can include emotional abuse tactics like gaslighting, humiliating, and isolating, which are harder to spot. If you have any suspicions of abuse, you need to set up individual assessment sessions. Without their partner present, and less fear of retribution, clients may feel safer disclosing what is really happening. It's also important that if you have a "no secrets" policy, that you reassure clients it does not apply to safety concerns, and that you will not disclose what they share with you to their partner.

To make it even more complicated, people in generally healthy couples may sometimes demonstrate behaviors that fall under the umbrella of emotional abuse, such as yelling, swearing, belittling, stonewalling, and even gaslighting. When in distress, people will resort to extreme measures to be heard by their partners. When this is the case, the key part of your assessment is to determine whether these behaviors are part of a *pattern* of abuse where one partner is attempting to manipulate, isolate, demean, and control their partner.

Therapist Reference

Assessing for Abusive Relationships

If you're concerned a new couple may be in an abusive relationship, here are some critical questions to ask yourself and your clients. If you answered yes to one or more of these questions, you should conduct a more in-depth assessment and seek supervision before continuing to work with the couple.

Ask yourself:

- Is there a power dynamic where one partner has control?
- Do any partners appear afraid? Have they been demeaned or isolated in this relationship? Have you seen them treated this way in session?
- Does the transgressing partner appear remorseful or interested in changing their behavior?
- Does the transgressing partner blame their partner and refuse to take responsibility? Do they claim their partner is actually the one being abusive?
- Is the transgressing partner accepting the blame for "making" their partner act out against them?
- Finally, do you have a gut feeling that this relationship is abusive?

Ask your clients (in individual sessions):

- Have you ever felt afraid for your safety in this relationship?
- Has your partner ever threatened or attempted to hurt you?
- Has your partner used their physical presence to intimidate you, such as blocking your path, throwing items, or hitting walls near you?
- Has your partner belittled, berated, embarrassed, isolated, controlled, or physically harmed you?
- Has anyone in your life expressed concern about this relationship or your safety after you've told them what happens during conflicts?
- Do you feel you deserve to be treated poorly or hurt?
- Does your partner keep you from spending time with your friends or family?
- Does your partner blame you for "making them" act in certain ways?

Untreated Substance or Mental Health Issues

If one partner has an active and untreated substance use issue, or if they have a significant and untreated mental health issue, they are likely not a good candidate for couples or sex therapy. These presenting problems must be treated first, or they will interfere with the couple's ability to work on their relationship. One concern is that any discomfort or distress caused by couples or sex therapy could exacerbate a client's substance use or mental health issue, which would then negatively impact the relationship, making couples therapy counterproductive and harmful. Clients who are struggling with a substance or mental health issue but are actively and effectively treating it may be able to participate in couples work productively, but they will also need adequate support and coping strategies outside of your sessions, such as individual therapy, support groups, and strong self-care skills.

Ongoing Affairs

Another important contraindication is if a client is having an ongoing affair. Many couples come to therapy to heal from infidelity, but couples therapy is not effective if the cheating is continuing. The client in the affair must decide if they want to work on their relationship or if they want to be with the affair partner; only then can the couples work start. Most of the time couples will seek treatment after discovering an affair and deciding they want to work on healing together, but this is not always the case. There are times when the unfaithful wants both—to stay in the relationship *and* to stay with the affair partner. They may be "hedging" by keeping contact with the affair partner in case couples therapy is not effective in healing and improving their current relationship. It's also possible that the unfaithful partner is truly, painfully torn—despite genuine interest in being in couples therapy, they cannot fully engage in the process because they haven't let go of the affair partner. Either way, if you suspect the affair may not be fully over, you should schedule individual sessions to learn more.

Insufficient Motivation

A lack of motivation to change indicates couples therapy will not be helpful. Couples need to have some degree of openness to engaging in self-reflection, taking responsibility, and making changes. While they may be focused on their partner as the problem, they still have to show a willingness to see how they may contribute to the issues in the relationship. Motivation can admittedly be hard to assess at first; showing up for a session indicates at least some interest in working on the relationship. However, sometimes you'll see a couple for a few sessions and realize that one partner begrudgingly agreed to attend therapy, perhaps because of an ultimatum, but is not actually interested in self-reflecting, taking responsibility, increasing empathy, or changing their behaviors. For these couples, there is little you can do besides carefully bringing attention to this barrier.

Therapist Reference

Contraindications Assessment

During a consultation and the intake sessions with a couple, ask yourself the questions below to see if the couple may have any contraindications for treatment. If you answer yes to some of these questions, especially to several questions within the same category, you should assess whether this couple is a good fit for therapy. You may want to do more individual sessions or seek out supervision as a part of this assessment.

Risk of violence or abuse:

- ☐ Does a partner report feeling afraid or unsafe in the relationship?
- ☐ Have the partners engaged in physical violence at any time?
- ☐ Does the transgressing partner blame the other partner for "making them" engage in these behaviors?
- ☐ Does the transgressing partner express no remorse for their actions, even after engaging in harmful or abusive behaviors?
- ☐ Does a partner appear disinterested in finding better ways to communicate and interact?
- ☐ Does the transgressing partner not see their abusive behaviors as ineffective, hurtful, and problematic, even when you explicitly point that out to them?

Untreated substance abuse or mental health issues:

- ☐ Does a partner report difficulty moderating their substance use?
- ☐ Do explosive fights occur only when one or all partners are under the influence?
- ☐ Does a partner express an unwillingness to curb or discontinue substance use?
- ☐ Have others (including those in the relationship) expressed serious concern about a partner's substance use?
- ☐ Does a partner have a mental health issue, diagnosed or not, that interferes with their ability to function? If diagnosed, do they deny the diagnosis as accurate or refuse to seek help?

- ☐ Is a partner receiving ineffective or insufficient treatment for a mental health issue?
- ☐ Are issues within the relationship caused or significantly worsened by a partner's mental health issue for which they are not in treatment?

Ongoing affairs:

- ☐ Has a partner reported an affair and not explicitly confirmed that it's over?
- ☐ Is a partner concerned (perhaps with some evidence) that the affair is ongoing?
- ☐ If the affair is "officially" over, does the unfaithful partner express continued interest in and attachment to the affair partner, indicating they are not truly committed to that relationship being over?

Insufficient motivation:

- ☐ Does a partner willfully refuse to engage in sessions by not speaking, mocking the process, or blaming their partner for everything?
- ☐ Did a partner share (perhaps during an individual session) that they are only there because their partner threatened to leave them if they didn't come to couples therapy?

Managing Secrets in Couples Work

Confidentiality is different for couples work because there are three or more people involved in the therapeutic relationship. As the therapist, you don't want to be in the habit of holding clients' secrets. This is because secrets are often barriers to progress, creating an uneven alliance where the other partner is in the dark about something important. But not all secrets are created equal. If the secret would significantly impact the work, then it's something that should be disclosed. But if you have individual sessions, you will undoubtedly get private information that you should keep confidential. For example, one partner may admit to having considered divorce recently or share that they have a sexual preference their partner knows nothing about; these secrets are not destructive if held by the therapist. Rather, it's important that you know this information so that you can better understand the feelings and needs of each client and support them in identifying and reaching their goals for the relationship.

How do you know when to keep a secret and when to encourage disclosure? The best marker is if the secret will be a clear barrier to the work. Affairs, acute untreated substance abuse, mental health issues, and clear disinterest in being in the relationship all fit into that category. Beyond that, research shows you'll need to use your judgment about whether disclosure is necessary depending on the couple and the secret (Mark & Schuman, 2020). There are many ethical gray areas when it comes to couples work, and you shouldn't hesitate to seek a second opinion. When in doubt, seek consultation; better yet, seek out supervision.

If the nature of the secret leads you to determine that therapy is contraindicated, you have a few options. First, you can try to resolve the contraindication, such as helping a client seek care for an untreated disorder or end an affair and disclose it to their partner. Second, you can discontinue treatment with the couple, explaining that therapy would not be helpful given their current circumstances. This can get complicated when you're terminating treatment due to a secret, as the other partner may not understand your reasons for ending therapy. In this scenario, when you don't want to disclose the reason, it's best to keep it high-level and say that you believe individual therapy will be more helpful at this time.

Termination

Terminating treatment occurs when the therapy has met its goals or when other circumstances force an early or abrupt termination (e.g., client moving out of your license's jurisdiction, discovery of a contraindication). Early or abrupt terminations due to circumstances like these are quicker and require the transmission of important information, such as why the therapy must end and how the couple can find new or further support in meeting their goals. Terminating after a successful treatment is a longer process that can help couples consolidate gains made in therapy, feel confident moving forward without treatment, and have a positive ending to a good therapeutic relationship.

If you must terminate therapy early for circumstantial or clinical reasons, be clear to your clients about the reasons for ending treatment. If it's because of contraindications, you should recommend a treatment plan for them to pursue and explain when they may be a good candidate for couples work (e.g., a partner with a substance abuse issue should seek individual therapy or join a sobriety group and return to couples therapy when the substance use is well managed). If termination is due to circumstantial reasons, such as a couple moving out of state, you should also make every effort to help them find a new therapist so they can continue their work. For couples who have completed their work and met their goals, you'll have the opportunity for a more in-depth termination discussion and process.

Some therapists set a termination date with their clients, agreeing that this will be the last session of the treatment. Others do a "step down" approach, where couples come less frequently over time, reducing therapy from weekly to biweekly to monthly, until they feel confident ending altogether. There is no right or wrong approach, and what you decide to offer will depend on your clinical orientation, availability, and flexibility.

Terminating therapy is an opportunity to consolidate the gains the couple has made over the course of treatment. It is a chance to reflect on where they were at the start of therapy, noting the insights and skills they've gained over the course of treatment. Identify how they have learned to navigate challenging conversations or issues, highlighting the specific skills they now have. For example, you can discuss how they choose to be open and curious in the face of their partner's complaint instead of being defensive, and how this has allowed for connection and a deeper understanding of the other. Reinforce the progress they have made together and individually, and highlight the areas they can continue to work on.

Another important takeaway from termination is helping the couple feel confident moving forward without sessions. Many are hesitant to stop therapy, especially when it's been successful, as they worry they may resume old patterns and lose their progress without you, their "referee," keeping watch. This is a time to reassure them of three things. First, remind them that they have learned and integrated new interactional patterns that are already happening outside of therapy. Consolidating their gains will help instill confidence that they can continue to communicate and connect without therapy. Second, let them know that they will inevitably resume old patterns, but if they are able to identify and change these patterns, they are still doing great. Every couple fights and even couples who "know better" sometimes resort to old patterns. Reassure them that everyone is a "work in progress," and that striving for growth and health is the most important aim. Indeed, the goal is not to prevent conflict or never engage in old, less productive communication and coping strategies, but rather to identify and repair when this does happen. Helping your clients anticipate that they can "go back to the old ways" or "do things wrong" and still be in a healthy relationship, as long as they process and repair effectively, will help lower their anxiety. Finally, give your clients the peace of mind that they can always come back to therapy if they need a refresher.

Finally, with the termination of therapy, it is important to show couples how to end a relationship on good terms, with a positive ending. This models what healthy goodbyes look like and makes it more likely that your clients will feel comfortable returning to therapy in the future, should they need to. Despite the good work you did together, there's always the possibility their relationship does not last forever. The hope is that if they need or want to end their relationship, they will do so with care and preserve the possibility of being on good terms.

Summary

This chapter covered a lot of ground. You've learned about key aspects of couples and sex therapy, establishing rapport and repairing ruptures, working through biases, managing intense affect, completing assessments, identifying contraindications for therapy, and navigating termination. For some of you, this information may be a review of previously learned knowledge; for others, this volume of information may feel overwhelming. Remember, this is just an introduction to these critical concepts—you are not expected to be an expert or feel fully confident yet. Feel free to reread this section as needed to ground yourself in the fundamentals of your work with couples.

CHAPTER 2

Theoretical Underpinnings

As with individual therapy, there are many evidence-based and burgeoning approaches to working with couples. In this section, you'll learn about some of the foremost orientations of couples and sex therapy. This will give you a general sense of the different approaches and point you in the direction of any trainings or certifications you may want to pursue in the future. It's helpful to know that many orientations have significant overlap in central tenets and interventions, and they are not mutually exclusive in how they approach couples work.

The information from chapter 1 remains true regardless of the orientations you may choose to pursue. They all rely on the therapist having a strong understanding of how the therapeutic alliance works with more than two people in the room, being confident and in control of sessions, ruling out contraindications, and being cognizant of their own biases.

Theories of Couples Therapy

Although there are numerous kinds of couples therapy, this chapter will provide brief descriptions of seven types: behavioral couples therapy, integrative behavioral couples therapy, emotionally focused couples therapy, insight-oriented couples therapy, Imago relationship therapy, Gottman Method couples therapy, and relational life therapy. Some newer forms for couples therapy have not been sufficiently researched and cannot be called evidence-based yet, whereas others have had years (even decades) of studies validating their efficacy. A 2022 review by Doss and colleagues looked at all published studies on couples therapies from 2010 to 2019 and found that four orientations qualified as "well-established:" behavioral couples therapy, cognitive behavioral couples therapy, emotionally focused therapy, and integrative behavioral couples therapy. Others, such as Imago relationship therapy, are possibly effective but require additional research. Gottman Method couples therapy is based on its own research and continues to be studied for efficacy, and relational life therapy is in the early stages of research to validate it as an effective method. It's important to note the majority of the research only looks at the efficacy of these orientations when treating monogamous, cisgender, heterosexual couples. However, research and resources continue to develop to support all types of couples, and studies have indicated that well-established couples therapy approaches are effective for the diverse population of couples that exist (Allan & Johnson, 2017; Zuccarini & Karos, 2011; Garanzini et al., 2017; Edwards et al., 2023).

Couples therapy began like all therapy did—with psychoanalytic roots. In the 1930s, some practicing therapists used psychoanalytic techniques to help couples discover and address their neurotic tendencies and unconscious desires, but the focus was on helping the individual partners improve their health, not changing the dynamic of their relationship (Gurman & Snyder, 2011). Three decades later, family therapy emerged as an expanding field, including some research and treatment models for how to help couples in the context of the family. Still, even after many famous family therapists began using these models to work with couples apart from the family, it wasn't until the mid-1980s that couples therapy became its own distinct field within the clinical psychology world. With the rise of new orientations, including emotionally focused couples therapy and behavioral couples therapy, couples became the focus of research and treatment. Each orientation has its own guiding principle of the source of issues within a couple, but many have overlapping conclusions and interventions. As the field continues to expand, more orientations are becoming evidence-based, and new perspectives continue to emerge.

One of the early forms of couples therapy was *behavioral couples therapy*, which looked at how behavioral changes could improve a marriage. The belief was that successful marriages had more positive interactions than negative ones, and the first iteration of this orientation had couples write down desired behaviors they'd like to see from their partner so they could explicitly request these behavioral changes (Stuart, 1969). Later, the orientation incorporated teaching communication skills, then integrating the ways that cognitive appraisals of one's partner impact the behavioral change, and finally turning into *cognitive behavioral couples therapy* (Epstein & Baucom, 2002). In the mid-1990s, this orientation evolved once more to include emotion regulation skills training and to promote acceptance and appreciation for one's partner as they make changes, which led to its relabel as *integrative behavioral couples therapy* (Jacobson & Christensen, 1996).

Emotionally focused couples therapy (EFCT), pioneered by Sue Johnson, took a different approach. Founded on the belief that all humans have an intrinsic need for secure, safe, loving connections starting with our attachments to our caregivers (Bowlby, 1969; Ainsworth et al., 1971), EFCT posits that attachment distress is the underlying cause of relational problems, as it leads to couples getting stuck in a negative cycle of behavioral patterns (Greenberg & Johnson, 1988). The negative cycle is fueled by painful, vulnerable feelings and fears related to attachment distress and longing. Caught between the wish to protect themselves from these painful feelings and to stabilize a relationship when the attachment feels threatened, clients engage in behaviors that actually serve to further separate the couple. These actions cause more distress in each partner, and they engage in more protective behaviors, leading to a self-sustaining cycle. In EFCT, the work lies in helping clients identify their attachment needs and the underlying feelings that lead to the protective responses. In this process, couples heal and strengthen their attachments through disclosing important feelings or needs and experiencing empathy and acceptance from their partner. Decades of research have validated EFCT as an effective and evidence-based method for helping couples (Wiebe & Johnson, 2016; Beasley & Ager, 2019).

Insight-oriented couples therapy is an evolution of the original psychoanalytic approach to treating couples. It seeks to promote affective restructuring by helping clients identify how prior relationships influence their current one. The belief behind this therapy is that uncovering assumptions, relationship narratives, coping mechanisms, and emotional responses to others (Snyder, 1999) will empower clients to choose more effective ways of engaging, instead of continuing to enact unconscious patterns. Insight-oriented couples therapy has been termed "possibly efficacious" in helping couples (Doss et al., 2022).

Imago relationship therapy, developed by Harville Hendrix and Helen LaKelly Hunt, is similarly based on the belief that feelings and experiences from our earliest relationships resurface and impact our adult romantic relationships. Imago therapy goes further by positing that people unconsciously seek out partners who are similar to those early relationships, allowing them to heal prior wounds (Hendrix et al., 2015). Imago therapy has limited research showing its efficacy (Doss et al., 2022).

Gottman Method couples therapy was developed by John Gottman, whose research at the Gottman Love Lab found key identifiers of couples who would have long, happy marriages and couples who would have marriages that deteriorate into resentment, disconnection, or divorce. Today, after just fifteen minutes spent observing a couple, Gottman can predict the ultimate outcome of a marriage with a 91 percent accuracy rate. His research led to the development of the Gottman Method, which uses psychoeducation and practice to help couples communicate and connect more effectively. Some key interventions are helping couples build "love maps," where they gain deeper understanding of each other, increase positive interactions, learn a three-step strategy for managing conflict, and create shared meaning and purpose (Gottman & Silver, 2015).

Relational life therapy (RLT), created by Terry Real, is a newer approach to couples work. The Relational Life Institute is in the process of conducting and publishing research to earn evidence-based status, but it is foundationally similar to Internal Family Systems therapy, a well-established model that looks at how different internal "parts" interact and determine our behavior. RLT incorporates parts language to help clients identify their wounded child, adaptive child, and wise adult-selves. Clients are encouraged to recognize how their family of origin has impacted them, particularly how their caregivers have hurt their wounded inner child and what defense mechanisms the adaptive child developed to protect that child. The goal is for clients to be intentional in their interactions, choosing to be the wise adult when engaging with their partner so they can avoid prior maladaptive responses and use more effective strategies for communication (Real, 2022). RLT takes a direct approach to couples work by helping clients take responsibility for their contribution to the current problem. RLT therapists are empathic but explicit as they label unproductive behaviors and call clients to change.

Theories of Sex Therapy

Since its inception, the field of sex therapy has suffered from a lack of theoretical backbone (Money, 1988). Subject to the theoretical zeitgeist, as were many topics in psychotherapy, sexual dysfunction was conceptualized in a psychoanalytic framework for the first half of the twentieth century (Edwards & Coleman, 2004). Within this framework, sexual challenges were viewed as the result of unresolved intrapsychic conflicts from childhood and successful treatment involved bringing those unconscious conflicts into the consciousness. It was thought that resolving the intrapsychic conflicts would resolve the sexual dysfunction.

It wasn't until the publication of Masters and Johnson's *Human Sexual Inadequacy* in 1970 that more behavioral techniques were introduced to the field of sex therapy. Based on their eleven years of research, Masters and Johnson (as cited in Edwards & Coleman, 2004) developed a brief, directive, and problem-focused method of treating sexual problems. Rather than the result of intrapsychic conflict, sexual challenges were interpreted as resulting from the combination of a sexually repressed upbringing and anxiety about sexual encounters. In essence, this model relied on learning, and the principal agent of change was re-education. In the years following, Helen Singer Kaplan's (1974) work expanded on this learning model by incorporating both direct, symptom-focused behavioral techniques as well as intrapsychic and interpersonal factors.

Despite these psychodynamic and behavioral models, the field of sex therapy still fell short in addressing some of the problems faced by clients. *Systemic sex therapy* ultimately emerged from this gap. In systemic treatments, "the role of the partner is considered in the creation, continuation, and correction of the problem" (Hertlein et al., 2009, pp. 75–76). Here, the couple is considered a system, and the sexual challenge is created by that system rather than residing in the individual.

Current theoretical frameworks expand on systemic theory and tend to be multidisciplinary in nature. In particular, due to the complexity of sexual issues, biopsychosocial models now include the following information as part of the assessment process: the client's medical history (medical model); intrapsychic conflict (psychodynamic model); social learning, cognitions, and beliefs (Masters and Johnson's *Human Sexual Inadequacy*); partner relationships (systemic sex therapy); and psychological well-being, family beliefs, subjective sexual experience, and external stressors. Within this multidisciplinary model, several treatment models have flourished, including trauma-informed treatment, mindfulness-based cognitive behavioral therapy, and EFCT.

Pursuing Further Training

Being a relatively young field, sex therapy is still searching for its theoretical footing. In short, there is no comprehensive, one-size-fits-all theory of sexual issues. Even as advances in theory and treatment have led to the expansion of the conceptual framework, moving toward more holistic and multidisciplinary approaches, sex therapy remains a burgeoning field with much research and refinement left to be done. No doubt more studies will be published before this book reaches your hands, and there will always be updated information to consume. We encourage you to never stop reading and learning. Chapter 11 will provide guidance and recommendations for additional resources, training, and certifications you can pursue to deepen your understanding and strengthen your practice.

Therapist Reflection

Reflections on Approaches to Couples and Sex Therapy

You have learned about several orientations to couples and sex therapy. There are many commonalities among them, though their theoretical foundations may differ. As you consider pursuing this work, we invite you to reflect on the following questions.

Was any of this information new to you? What are your reactions to learning that couples and sex therapy is still a new field of work in psychology?

____

____

____

Which orientation of couples or sex therapy resonated most with you? Why?

____

____

____

Would you want to pursue one of these orientations for further education and training?

____

____

____

Do you think you want to take a more psychoanalytic or psychodynamic approach to your work with couples, or will you be a more psychoeducational and skills-based therapist?

____

____

____

Given that most of the research only looks at heterosexual, cisgender monogamous couples, what questions do you have about how the work might be different with couples who have other gender identities, sexual orientations, or relationship structures?

___

___

___

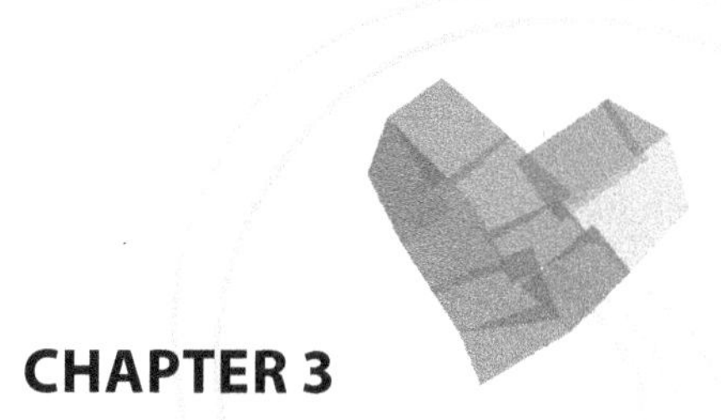

CHAPTER 3

Attachment Theory and the Negative Cycle

This book exists because romantic relationships are important to us. Humans are hardwired for connection, first with caregivers and family, then with friends and romantic partners (Ainsworth, 1971; Bowlby, 1969; Greenberg & Johnson, 1988). Our relationships give us happiness and meaning and are even linked to living longer lives. Knowing this, it's no wonder we experience intense distress when our relationships feel unstable (Hart, 2023).

As we briefly introduced in the previous chapter, we all have the need for security, safety, and connections—this was provided (or not provided) by our early caregivers. Attachment theory was pioneered by John Bowlby (1969) as he studied this connection between mother and child. The infants in his study sought closeness to their mothers and were distressed when faced with separation. His work was continued by Mary Ainsworth (1971), who looked at how infant response to being separated from caregivers could indicate the security of their attachment. This concept was later applied to romantic relationships; relational distress, whether it presents as frequent loud arguments or icy withdrawal, is evidence of a threatened attachment that all partners are eager to repair.

Attachment Theory

Attachment theory posits that humans learn how to form attachments (and what kind of attachments we can expect to have) from our early relationships with our caregivers—usually our parents. These relationships give us blueprints for how to interact in future close relationships. Specifically, your clients' relationships with their caregivers have implicitly taught them what they can expect from their romantic partners (Greenberg & Johnson, 1988), giving them answers to questions such as:

- What can you expect from people in terms of communication or empathy?
- How do you anticipate people will respond to conflict or confrontation?

- Do you need to behave in certain ways to keep others happy because you worry that not being agreeable or compliant will make them leave?
- Do you feel you need to protect yourself from being taken advantage of by other people?
- Can you rely on the people you're closest with to repair after conflict or do fights mean the end of the relationship?

If a client's parents were responsive, caring, and consistent, the client may think future partners will also provide the same reliable love and care. This is especially true if their parents remained this way even when their child was angry, sad, or overwhelmed; this meant those negative emotions weren't too much for their parents to handle, and they were able to love and care for their child even when the child was at their most upset. This type of child-parent relationship leads to a secure attachment style.

However, if their parents were inconsistent in their care and affection, if they got annoyed or stressed by the child's needs, or if they were neglectful or abusive, your clients may have learned a much different lesson. They may expect romantic partners to be unreliable and harsh, or they may think their negative feelings will push people away. This type of experience results in an insecure attachment style, of which there are three subtypes; you will learn about all the attachment styles in the next section.

Helping clients to identify and understand their attachment style can normalize the patterns, recurring behaviors, and fears they've experienced in their romantic relationships. It can also empower them to see opportunities for unlearning unhelpful expectations and moving toward developing more secure attachments with their partners.

The Four Types of Attachment Styles

Secure

If a client has a *secure* attachment, they have high self-esteem and a strong sense of stability in relationships, enjoy and seek out relationships, share their feelings freely, can tolerate relationships ending, and are generally relationally resilient. They believe that people are usually reliable, trustworthy, and loving in relationships. They assume the best in their partner, and if their partner does disappoint them, they're able to manage those feelings and address them openly. When fights do happen, they don't see them as the end of the world or an annoyance; they look at fights as being part of any healthy relationship and something that can be worked through with their partner. They have a clear sense of their needs and values and seek out partners who are able to treat them with love and respect.

Anxious-Preoccupied

If a client has an *anxious-preoccupied* (or anxious) attachment style, they crave closeness with their partner and feel pretty anxious if their partner seems distant. They prioritize their partner's needs over their own as a way of keeping their partner happy—a skill they learned early on in life. Because they likely have low self-esteem and feel insecure, they may be jealous or possessive, and probably seek frequent reassurance that things are okay in the relationship. They may feel responsible for any relationship issue that arises and also feel responsible for fixing things, even if that means apologizing when they did nothing wrong. They hate when their partner is unhappy because they usually assume they're unhappy with *them* (and not about something else, like work). They fear that any tension or problem might make their partner leave.

Dismissive-Avoidant

If a client has a *dismissive-avoidant* (or avoidant) attachment style, they are probably quite independent and have a hard time letting people get close to them. In order to feel safe, they like to maintain some space from their partner. Their caregivers probably didn't show them much love or affection beyond meeting their basic needs, so they learned not to depend on other people for emotional closeness. They might pull away if their partner tries to get close, keep secrets or maintain other parts of their life separate from their partner, and even abruptly end the relationship when it feels too stressful or complicated. They may find their partner's needs and feelings frustrating or taxing, and they wish their partner would deal with things on their own without involving them (just like they do!). The self-sufficiency that is a great strength of theirs can also make it hard for people to get close to them. They feel overwhelmed dealing with conflict and have a hard time imagining how people can fight and then move forward together; to them it feels like conflicts inevitably mean the relationship will end.

Fearful-Avoidant

If a client has a *fearful-avoidant* (disorganized) attachment style, they tend to shift between anxious and dismissive styles. They most likely have a history of trauma that has taught them that important people in their life will be neglectful, selfish, mean, uncaring, or abusive. As a result, they find relationships to be confusing and chaotic. They may exhibit abusive behaviors, such as being controlling, dismissive, distrusting, or explosive toward their partner without explanation. They want closeness but don't know how to get it, so they pull their partner in tight then suddenly push them away when they feel afraid of losing them or become worried that they'll get hurt. Despite this behavior, they still want to have close, meaningful relationships (all humans do!). It goes without saying that having this attachment style puts them in a tough place; they seek closeness but can't maintain it.

Determining Attachment Style

Knowing your clients' attachment styles gives you a framework for understanding them and helping them determine how to grow. By gathering a relationship history during your intake, you can begin to assess your clients' attachment styles. Look for patterns in how their relationships start, what common problems they experience, and how their relationships end. You can also refer your clients to take an attachment style assessment. Some clients will come in knowing their attachment style, but keep in mind that self-assessments are inherently biased and can be inaccurate. You should make your own determination of your clients' attachment styles.

If your clients discover they have an attachment style other than secure and are worried about this, please reassure them that attachment styles are *not* permanent (Kirkpatrick & Hazan, 1994). Your clients may have developed habitual ways of interacting in their relationships, but those styles can be changed as they build self-esteem and emotion regulation skills and choose to respond differently in their relationships. In the literature, the term *earned-secure* is used to describe people who developed an insecure attachment style after negative experiences with caregivers but were later able to establish a secure way of forming bonds (Roisman et al., 2002).

The following chart includes key features of each attachment style. You can share this with your clients or use it for your own assessment.

Features of Attachment Styles

	Secure	Anxious-Preoccupied	Dismissive-Avoidant	Fearful-Avoidant
Self-esteem	Strong and stable	Varying; can be low	Varying; can be low	Inconsistent but generally low
Response to conflict	Sees it as an opportunity and not the end of the world; is able to work through issues with partner	Feels scared that conflict will be the end of the relationship; wants to fix things as soon as possible	Feels frustrated and overwhelmed by conflict and withdraws during serious conversations or fights	Engages in frequent conflict but is distressed by it; doesn't know how to have calm arguments

Desired level of closeness	Wants healthy balance of closeness and separateness	Wants lots of closeness and connection; thinks this will keep partner from leaving	Can get uncomfortable with too much emotional intensity; prefers autonomy and self-sufficiency	Wants closeness but feels scared when it happens; doesn't know how to maintain closeness without feeling vulnerable
Relationship with caregivers	Caregivers were loving and responsive	Caregivers' affection was dependent on good behavior and acquiescence	Caregivers met basic needs (food, shelter, etc.) but otherwise gave little affection	Caregivers were inconsistent and likely neglectful or abusive
Romantic history	Many healthy relationships, both long and short, with fairly amicable endings	May have intense relationships with breakups that feel like the end of the world	May have shorter relationships with quick endings	Chaotic, intense, and volatile relationships

The Impact of Previous Romantic Relationships

Just as attachment style influences how your clients create and sustain relationships, they have also been impacted by their previous romantic relationships. Unhealthy prior relationships may have given them the wrong idea of what they can expect from their partners and what healthy conflict or communication looks like. In contrast, if they have generally had positive and healthy relationships, they are more likely to know their worth in a relationship, have reasonable expectations for their partners, communicate their needs and feelings, navigate conflict, and even end relationships in a healthy manner.

It's important to note that people with a secure attachment style are likely to be negatively impacted by bad relationships because they have a foundational sense of what healthy relationships are, whereas someone with one of the insecure styles will be more affected because any negative experience will reinforce their unhelpful beliefs about people, whether it's the belief that people will leave if they aren't perfect or the belief that they need to be vigilant in relationships to protect themselves.

To gain a deeper understanding of how your clients' previous relationships have shaped who they are today as a romantic partner, invite them to complete the following client activity.

Client Activity

Identifying Internalized Messages and Beliefs from Prior Relationships

Write down all the meaningful relationships you've had in your life. It doesn't matter how young you were or how "serious" the relationship was; a middle school romance can have a bigger impact than a short relationship in our thirties, and a three year on-and-off again hookup can be more meaningful than a two-month "official" relationship. Avoid making any judgments about the relationship itself—simply list the meaningful relationships you've had, and then place a check mark next to the lessons or messages you've taken from each of them.

Relationships

____

____

____

Messages or Lessons Learned from Relationships

Self-esteem:

- ☐ No matter what I do, I'm never enough for my partners.
- ☐ My partners value who I am and what I bring to the relationship.
- ☐ I always feel like I'm doing more than my partners and that they aren't good enough for me.

Support:

- ☐ I can trust people to be there when I need them.
- ☐ People always let me down; I can only count on myself.
- ☐ It's not a good idea to ask partners for help or support—it will annoy them or make them leave.

Abandonment:

- ☐ People always betray or leave me no matter what I do.
- ☐ If people leave me, it's because the relationship wasn't right for them; it doesn't mean I won't find another person.
- ☐ People never leave me because I'll always leave first—it's how I protect myself from feeling rejected and hurt.

Conflict resolution:

- ☐ If there's a problem in the relationship, we can work through it, and it's good to talk about issues when they come up.
- ☐ Conflicts mean breakups; I've never been able to get through a really hard time with my partner before.
- ☐ I avoid conflicts at all costs, yet somehow my partner still gets angry with me; no matter what I do I feel like I'm always wrong.

Aligning goals:

- ☐ I can work with my partner to create shared goals or make compromises when possible.
- ☐ I need to give into my partner's goals, even if they directly conflict with what I want in life.
- ☐ I can't compromise my goals or I'll lose myself in the relationship; I'd rather my partner leave me than change my goals.

Negotiating needs:

- ☐ It's easiest if I just prioritize my partner's needs so that they'll be happy and stay; whenever I try to advocate for my own needs, it seems to go poorly.
- ☐ I can't sacrifice my needs in a relationship or I'll become a doormat, so I need to stand up for myself.
- ☐ I think our needs can be discussed and compromised in a way that feels okay, it just might take a little work.

Patterns You Notice in Your Relationships

Looking at your responses, take a moment to think about patterns you've identified in your prior romantic relationships. Ask yourself the following questions:

Do your relationships tend to last the same length of time?

____

____

____

Do they typically end in similar way?

____

____

____

Are you drawn to partners with similar personality traits or conflict styles?

____

____

____

Do you tend to see yourself or your partner as being ultimately to blame for conflict or dysfunction in the relationship?

____

____

____

Is it generally you or your partner who ultimately breaks things off?

____

____

____

Do you see any patterns in how your *partners* tend to act in your relationships?

Think back on the messages you've learned from your relationships—do you notice any common themes?

How do you think these messages could impact your role or security in your current or a future romantic relationship?

Are there any similarities between your romantic relationships and your relationship with your parents?

Common Roles

Depending on their attachment styles and relationship histories, your clients will fall into one of three roles: pursuer, withdrawer, or secure responder.

Pursuers

The *pursuer* actively seeks out closeness from their partner. They are distressed by disconnection and relationship insecurity and may try to reestablish the connection through a variety of actions. They often point out problems in the relationship or with their partner, hoping that raising the issues will help resolve them. They may unconsciously think, *My partner never hears how important problems are, so I'll get louder until they listen;* however, their urgent effort to address issues can feel overwhelming to their partners, leading to more tension or disconnection. Pursuers can be perceived as clingy, needy, critical, and impossible to satisfy.

Pursuers usually have an anxious attachment style. This makes sense, as people with this style dislike conflict and are quick to repair and reconnect. They feel anxious when their relationship is not in a state of harmony because they fear it will lead to the relationship continuing to disintegrate and eventually ending. They have a low tolerance for conflict due to deep-seated fears that they are always the one at fault, are inherently unlovable, and thus will ultimately be rejected and abandoned.

Withdrawers

In contrast to pursuers, withdrawers tend to pull back when conflict arises. They experience attachment distress as overwhelming and retreat into themselves in attempts to avoid the pain associated with disconnection. Withdrawers often feel that engaging in the conflict doesn't work, and whatever they do isn't enough or doesn't help, so they pull back entirely. In doing so, they are trying to reestablish some stability in the relationship. Withdrawers may think to themselves, *Whatever I say and do seems to make things worse, so if I don't say anything at all, maybe this problem will go away*; however, to their partner, the withdrawal can feel like a rejection and be perceived as indifference or a lack of care.

Withdrawers tend to have more of an avoidant attachment style. They dislike or don't know how to manage conflict with their loved ones. They're skilled at blocking the painful feelings that occur when they're disconnected from their partner by pulling away into a safe place where they can't be hurt by their partner's demands or criticisms. Withdrawers find their partner's emotions to be exhausting and can perceive their partner as impossible to please. This usually triggers underlying fears that the withdrawer is a disappointment or failure, making them want to retreat further from their partner. Because withdrawers are self-sufficient, they don't understand why their partner can't manage their own painful emotions on their own, just like they do.

Secure Responders

In addition to pursuers and withdrawers, there are also people with secure attachments who respond to conflict with calm curiosity. They don't attack, withdraw, or become defensive when their partner voices a need or concern. *Secure responders* can stay emotionally regulated and maintain their self-esteem during conflict. If their partner pursues or withdraws, they are aware of how this emotionally impacts them and have the skills to actively choose a helpful response instead of engaging in unhelpful behaviors that continue or escalate the conflict.

Most people coming into couples therapy do not respond in this way. Even people with a secure attachment and strong history of effectively managing conflict can be pulled into painful patterns that sustain disconnection. This can occur when, despite the best efforts of the securely attached person, their partner does not know how to engage in healthy communication and continues to attack or withdraw.

While these role distinctions are helpful for understanding how your clients behave in relationships, it's best to think of them as being on a spectrum—while people typically present as one specific role, that role can shift depending on their partner and the relationship dynamic. For example, someone may present as a pursuer in a relationship with a partner who is incredibly withdrawn, but they may seem secure in a relationship with a partner who has a greater ability to talk through conflict. Additionally, each role has a spectrum of behaviors and of varying acuity. For example, there are angry, aggressive pursuers, and there are softer, sadder ones. Be flexible as you consider what role your clients best fit, and always leave room for people to move toward a more securely attached role.

It's important to know that no matter which role your clients play, they are striving to achieve the same two goals: protecting themselves from painful feelings and attempting to preserve the relationship. Unfortunately, some behaviors tend to foster more emotional disconnection and can increase distress for the couple.

The Relationship Grid

Another way of looking at attachment and how your clients may respond during conflict is through the *relationship grid* developed by the RLT orientation to couples therapy. The grid's vertical axis represents self-esteem, from grandiosity at the top to shame at the bottom; healthy self-esteem resides within the middle of the axis. On the horizontal axis is the spectrum of boundaries, with the right side representing boundaryless behavior (often associated with a pursuer role) and the left side representing walled-off behavior (often associated with a withdrawer role) (Real, 2008).

*Relationship Grid**

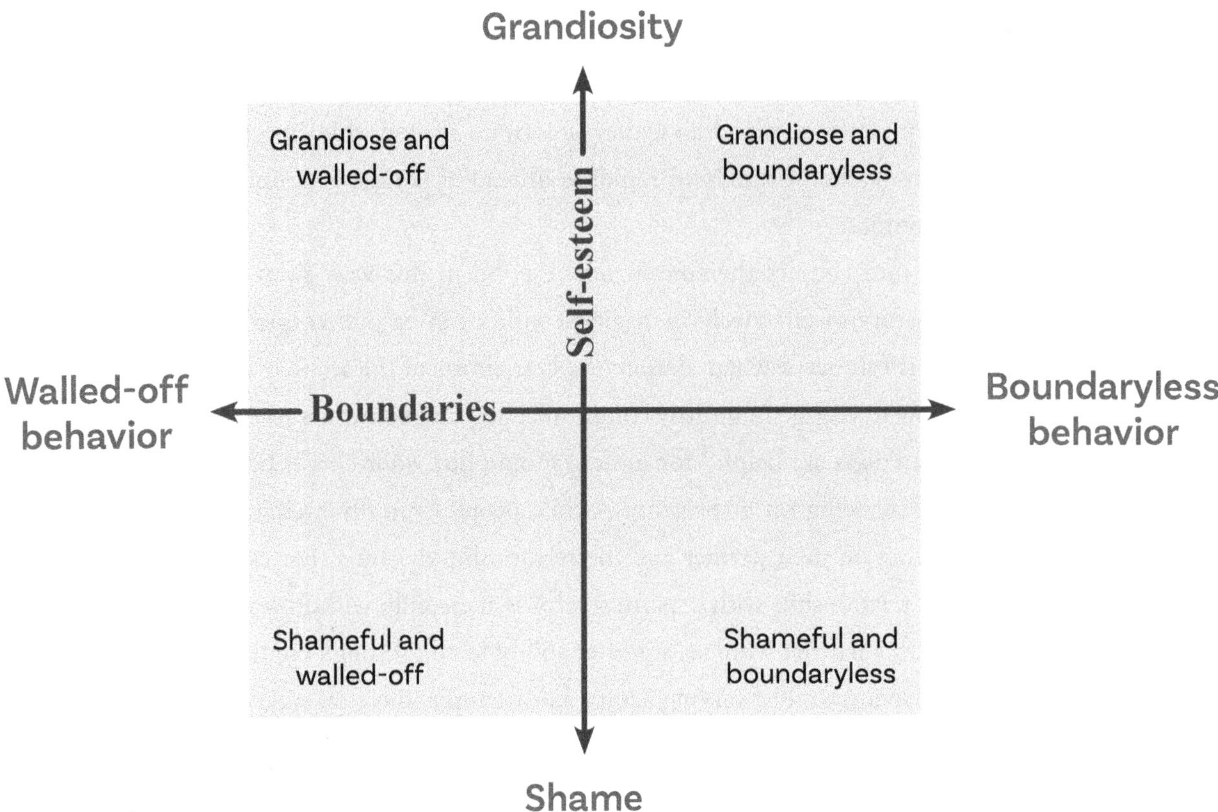

Shameful and Boundaryless

The lower right quadrant of the grid represents people with low self-esteem who exhibit boundaryless behaviors and thus are often perceived as needy and manipulative. RLT founder Terry Real (2008) explains that at the extreme end of this quadrant are "love addicts" (i.e., people who will do anything to get and keep a partner). Desperate to maintain the relationship, love addicts typically panic at the first sign of disconnection. Clients in this quadrant likely have an anxious attachment style and actively seek out closeness, even in ways that push their partner away.

Shameful and Walled-Off

The lower left quadrant represents people who feel terribly about themselves and disengage from their partners during fights. They think everything they do is wrong and feel deep shame about who they are; they don't want their partner to truly see them, lest the partner recognize how flawed they are and leave. People in this quadrant may be clinically depressed, but even without a diagnosis, their self-dislike makes them withdraw from their partner.

---

* This image is adapted from *The New Rules of Marriage* by Terrence Real, 2008, Ballentine Books.

Grandiose and Walled-Off

The upper left quadrant represents people with excessively high self-esteem who look down at their partners and stonewall them during conflict. These are the clients who engage in passive-aggressive behaviors and, at times, are just plain mean. They see themselves in an overly positive and forgiving light and won't let go of being "right" in an argument. Intent on proving their point and making their partner acquiesce, they are withholding and emotionally unreachable.

Grandiose and Boundaryless

The upper right quadrant is the one of most concerning, as clients in this part of the grid are at risk of being abusers. People who are grandiose and lack boundaries are the angry pursuers who see their partner as the problem and react strongly to every offense or disappointment. They tend to be controlling, manipulative, condescending, and harsh.

Clients may find it easier to find themselves in this grid than fully understand their attachment history and style, so it can be a helpful tool for you to use in assessment. It can inspire insight when clients realize how they feel and act during fights, and it can also provide critical clinical information for you if clients misidentify where they fall. It can also be important to see whether clients who fall in the upper right quadrant, where abusers usually do, show remorse or concern for being in this category.

Understanding the Negative Cycle

Every couple has a pattern to how their conflicts unfold. Each couples therapy orientation has its own framework and language when describing this. In EFCT it's referred to as the couple's "dance," or more clinically, "the negative cycle;" the vulnerable emotions and behavioral responses create a loop that keeps a couple in conflict. Gottman describes couples being "gridlocked" when they have recurring, ineffective, disconnecting conversations about perpetual problems (Gottman & Silver, 2015). And in RLT, it's explained as "the more, the more"—for example, the more one person yells, the more the other person falls silent.

EFCT sees attachment distress as the root cause of the conflict pattern, meaning that clients are feeling insecure and emotionally disconnected in their relationship (Greenberg & Johnson, 1988). When painful feelings are triggered, your clients' outward responses are intended to protect them from feeling unsafe or hurt. Often, these responses are also attempts at stabilizing or bolstering the relationship, even though it doesn't always feel that way to the other person (Johnson & Brubacher, 2016). In other words, behaviors may appear to be intentionally hurtful, but EFT sees them as attempts to soothe attachment distress and maintain the relationship.

The Gottman Institute has found that 69 percent of problems that couples face are perpetual and unsolvable, meaning that the couple will continue to face these problems throughout the lifetime of their relationship. Gottman & Silver (2015) also found that happy couples are ones who are able to communicate about these issues, accept that no one is "right" and that it doesn't have to be "solved," and maintain fondness even during challenging conversations. They explain that when couples are stuck in gridlock (i.e., the negative cycle), they are in "negative sentiment override," meaning everything said or done by one partner is taken in a negative way by the other. Even a benign comment in a neutral tone could be taken as angry or offensive when a couple is in negative sentiment override. Gottman Therapy has researched the specific behaviors that are evident when couples are stuck in this place, which include beginning conversations in a harsh way, flooding (or the fight-or-flight response, which will be discussed in chapter 4), failing repair attempts, and Gottman's Four Horsemen—the main predictors of divorce (defensiveness, stonewalling, criticism, and contempt, which will be discussed in chapter 5) (Gottman & Silver, 2015). This orientation looks at moving couples into positive sentiment override by helping them engage in healthier behaviors to create a solid foundation of friendship.

While the content of the fights may change, the patterns do not because the negative cycle underlies each conflict. Your clients will have similar painful feelings in each argument, and they will engage in similar protective behaviors in response to those feelings (which will correlate to the role they adopt: pursuer or withdrawer). For example, your clients may disagree about how to load the dishwasher one week and bicker about how they divide time between their families the next, but the emotional and behavioral cycle is the same. Identifying the negative cycle is critical because it will allow you and your clients to see beyond the content and move from solving one specific problem to understanding the more important issues at play.

Regardless of the theoretical orientation you use to understand a couple's patterns of conflict, it's important to know that they are self-sustaining. Once a couple has fallen into a negative cycle, it's very hard for them to get back out of it. Since vulnerable feelings are hard to tolerate, your clients are not eager to let go of the protective behaviors they've developed to numb those emotions. It is your job to help clients identify their protective (but unhelpful) behaviors as well as the vulnerable feelings they are trying to avoid by engaging in these behaviors; once the clients are more aware, you must help them choose a *new* way of engaging.

Identifying the Negative Cycles

Many couples who feel therapy is not helpful claim that each session focuses only on "the problem of the day" instead of helping them explore and change the negative cycle that lies at the root of their arguments. There are three common maladaptive cycles in relationships, each a different combination of the pursuer and withdrawer roles: attack-attack, withdraw-withdraw, and demand-withdraw. Identifying which of the negative cycles is in effect will allow you to help both partners address and heal the more important root cause of their unhappiness—and avoid getting stuck on specific details of disagreements.

Attack-Attack

As the name implies, attack is exactly what happens in this negative cycle. This is when two partners go on the offensive, arguing and pointing fingers at the other person. Each partner feels attacked and criticized and protects themself by returning the emotional assault. These arguments can escalate quickly and become explosive. Without one partner working to de-escalate and repair, significant emotional and relational damage can be done, and quickly.

Demand-Withdraw

This very common negative cycle occurs when a pursue and withdrawer get into a conflict. The pursuer makes a demand (e.g., for more time, for a change), pointing out issues and trying to get their partner to meet their needs. Their partner feels attacked and overwhelmed by the demand and emotionally withdraws, retreating into themselves where they feel safe from attack. The more the pursuer emphasizes their demand or adds to it, the more the withdrawer pulls back.

Withdraw-Withdraw

In this cycle, partners have proverbially thrown in the towel on trying to resolve conflicts. They don't express concerns or raise issues about the relationship. Their relationship may look peaceful to the outside observer, but underneath the calm exterior are partners who are stewing in resentment and feeling deeply disconnected, unhappy, helpless and hopeless.

The Cycle Is the Problem

As you learned in chapter 1, you, as the therapist, treat the *relationship* as your client. In doing so, you should treat the negative cycle as the problem. While it's true that some clients will exhibit behaviors that are inherently problematic and require specific intervention, the majority of the work is helping the clients see the unhelpful patterns as the issue and supporting them to address these patterns together (Greenberg & Johnson, 1988).

When couples say they want to improve their communication (a commonly cited reason for seeking therapy), what they mean is that they feel hurt or unheard when talking with their partner. That happens because they are protecting themselves—through being defensive, blaming, withdrawing, or some other action—and these protections are leading to disconnection by furthering the emotional distance and escalating conflict. Your goal is to help your clients see how their behaviors create a self-sustaining cycle that prevents them from connecting.

From this chapter, you now know how early relationships influence attachment style, and which attachment styles are correlated with roles that people often take in relationships during conflict. You know the goal is to help couples see their negative cycle as the problem they need to solve. In the next chapter, you'll explore how emotion regulation is critical for your clients to learn, as it provides a foundation from which they can do the harder work required in couples therapy.

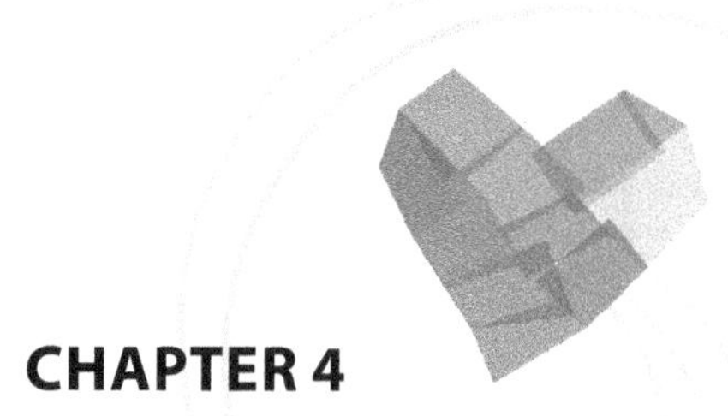

CHAPTER 4

Emotion Regulation and Coregulation

You've learned that conflict creates attachment distress and that this type of distress is inherently dysregulating. Even when couples can accept that conflict is inevitable in an intimate relationship, feeling insecure in a relationship can still lead to anxiety, panic, hopelessness, helplessness, and despair. Knowing how to recognize and manage those feelings is an essential skill for healthy relationships; it enables partners to calmly stay in tough conversations (instead of exploding or withdrawing) and communicate as effectively as possible. In order for your clients to navigate the most challenging moments of a relationship, they must learn to regulate their own emotions and tolerate their partner's emotions, establish and respect each other's boundaries, and identify the most effective ways of self-soothing.

This chapter will teach the critical emotion regulation skills your clients need to bring themselves back to their emotional baseline when they fight with their partner. It will explain what happens physiologically when a client is dysregulated, how they can identify that feeling, and what they can do about it. It also looks at the important relationship between emotion regulation and coregulation in relationships.

Emotion Regulation

Relationships are wonderful, but they are also emotionally dysregulating. Being close to someone else means that your clients will be vulnerable and will inevitably have their feelings hurt by that person. Although humans crave closeness, we can also struggle with it. Emotion regulation—that is, being able to manage difficult feelings such as anger, hurt, sadness, panic, or fear—is a critical skill for your clients to develop so that they can maintain close relationships without too much emotional distress.

It is important for clients to remember that their partner is not responsible for fixing their feelings. Each client is the only person who can change their own mood and regulate their feelings. Many people expect their partner to make them feel better, or to not make them upset in the first place. However, given that conflicts are inevitable in a close relationship, feeling hurt, sad, or angry at times is also inevitable. It's important for clients to understand that they are the only people who can manage those feelings when they arise. Of course, their partner can help in some ways, such as providing support or comfort, giving them space, or offering suggestions (more about this when we look at coregulation), but at the end of the day, each client is in charge of their own feelings.

Emotional Dysregulation

Some arguments are so intense or upsetting that your clients may feel overwhelmed by their feelings. In fact, this probably happens frequently. During these moments, your clients are emotionally *flooded* (Gottman & Silver, 2015) (i.e., in a state of high physiological arousal)—you may know it as the *fight-or-flight* response. This response is an adaptive survival response to a life-threatening situation. When faced with a life-threatening situation (think encountering an angry bear in the woods), the fight-or-flight response jumpstarts your clients' bodies into action so that they can protect and save themselves (as in run away from the bear).

However, this response can be triggered to non-life-threatening situations as well, such as a heated argument with a loved one. When this happens, the internal switch is flipped, putting your clients in survival mode. Unnecessary bodily functions, such as digestion, are turned off so that energy can be redirected elsewhere. Their eyes dilate, their heart starts beating faster, they sweat, and they breathe more heavily as their bodies prepare for fight or flight in response to the stressor.

The most important thing to know about the flooding or fight or flight is that when your clients are in this heightened state, they are not physically capable of listening or communicating as effectively (Gottman, 1993). Because resources are sent to parts of the body that will ensure survival (such as the heart and limbs so that the person can escape the situation), they are inevitably channeled away from other organs, including the brain. However, one crucial part of the brain does get activated in this scenario: the amygdala, a small structure in charge of processing fearful or threatening situations. The amygdala's activation turns off the prefrontal cortex—the brain structure in charge of higher order thinking, such as logic and reasoning. After all, a life-threatening situation doesn't call for calm, empathic thinking! In a conflict scenario, your clients' bodies are telling them they need focus and adrenaline to fight off an attack or to run as fast as they can.

The fight-or-flight response has been a life-saving adaptation in the survival of the human species. Nowadays, however, your clients aren't likely to encounter many bears that trigger this response. Instead, an intense argument with their partner is much more likely to cause their body to prepare for a life-threatening situation, even though they are physically safe. Remember that attachment distress makes people feel *emotionally* unsafe. It inspires fear that the person they love and count on isn't there for them, or that a rupture will turn into an ending. These fears feel intolerable and lead to panic. Recall that our attachment style is born from our relationship with early caregivers on whom we do literally depend for survival; because we could die without their care, a rupture in those relationships would understandably trigger fight or flight. Attachment distress in an adult romantic relationship, although not technically life-threatening, triggers the same response.

Emotional flooding is more common and more destructive in a relationship's earlier stages. Research shows couples generally experience less emotional flooding over time (Hooper et al., 2017). This could indicate that couples feel increased attachment security in their marriage, and thus conflicts do not stir up the same degree of attachment distress and emotional dysregulation. However, emotional flooding can prevent a couple from reaching that point, so learning emotional regulation and communication skills is essential. Provide the following client activity to introduce your clients to the signs they may be emotionally flooded.

Client Activity

Signs of Being Emotionally Flooded

It's important for you to know when you're in a flooded state (i.e., fight or flight) so that you can take a break from the conflict. For some people, being flooded feels like they're on the verge of a panic attack, where they can't control their breathing and the room starts to spin. For others, they may want to run out of the room or even end the relationship just to end the conflict. The following are the most common symptoms of a flooded state. Place a check mark on any of the symptoms that you've experienced during a conflict:

- ☐ Increased heart rate
- ☐ Sweaty palms
- ☐ Quick or irregular breathing
- ☐ Muscle tension
- ☐ Tightness in chest
- ☐ Difficulty tracking the conversation (feeling lost or confused)
- ☐ Changes in vision (tunnel vision or blurriness)
- ☐ Agitation and irritability
- ☐ Anger and frustration
- ☐ Fear or panic
- ☐ Emotional withdrawal
- ☐ Desire to escape the situation
- ☐ Desire to emotionally attack your partner

What are some other indications, either body-based feelings or thoughts that you have, that indicate you are feeling flooded during an argument?

____

____

____

What are signs (at least as far as you can tell) that your partner is feeling flooded?

____

____

____

Share these signs with your partner so that you both know what to look out for in yourself and the other person when you're in a tough conversation.

Self-Soothing

As you know, your clients need to be able to regulate their emotions when they're upset in order to effectively manage conflicts. If they're feeling flooded during a conversation with their partner(s) and it's time to take a break from it, they need to know some self-soothing techniques that can help them regain their emotional grounding and their capacity to think clearly.

Keep in mind that self-soothing activities may take some time before they work. When someone is flooded, their body releases hormones that lead to feeling stressed and activated, and it takes time for these hormones to be filtered back out. Your clients should give themselves 20 to 60 minutes of self-soothing before they expect to feel back to normal. Clients with trauma or difficulty self-regulating may need hours or even days before they can return to their emotional baseline. Encourage your clients to take all the time they need and not resume the conversation until they feel ready.

There are several easy, evidence-based options for self-soothing that can help your clients return to their emotional baseline, no matter where they are or what they're doing.

- Deep breathing has been shown to stimulate the parasympathetic nervous response, the opposite response of fight or flight. When your clients engage in deep breathing exercises, their heart rate will slow down, their blood pressure will drop, and their anxiety will decrease. This will allow their body to reallocate resources to the brain, improving their ability to listen, process information, and communicate. There are many methods for practicing deep breathing that you can teach your clients to use, both at home and even during a session.
- Grounding strategies involve clients using their five senses to recenter, or ground, themselves. For example, they can look around the room and focus on a single item, pay attention to the sensation of their body sitting in the chair and their feet rooted on the floor, focus on the soothing scent of a candle, or even take a hot or cold shower. For clients with trauma histories, grounding strategies will be especially important for preventing or treating dissociation during session.
- If a client needs to take a longer break from the argument, they can try changing their environment, especially through going outside or exercising. Being in nature helps us get a bigger perspective on life and pulls us out of the narrow moment we're feeling consumed by. Exercise is a guaranteed way to reset the nervous system by expending the anxious energy that builds up when we feel flooded.

Self-Soothing in Action

No matter how securely attached someone is or how strong their coping mechanisms, everyone experiences emotional flooding. To better understand what this experience feels like and how to use self-soothing strategies, imagine for a moment that you are one of your clients learning to manage heightened emotions in your relationship. One day, your partner comes home and makes an offhand comment about how they almost tripped over your shoes when they walked in because you left them right in front of the door. Innocuous enough, right? But what they don't know is that you've had a stressful day at work and were already feeling emotionally fragile. Their comment pushes you over the edge and you feel attacked, criticized, and not good enough at work or at home. You feel your heart rate rise and you want to explode in defense of yourself:

"You leave your shoes there all the time! How hard is it to look down when you walk anyway? I always put them on the shoe rack and this *one* time I forget you have to make a big deal out of it!"

But instead of saying that, you take a deep breath. You do a few more deep, slow breaths until you feel your heart rate slowing down. You look at your dog, excited to see you, and give him a pet while noticing how soft his fur is. You smell the dinner your partner has been cooking and feel a rush of appreciation for having a warm meal made for you.

Once you feel calmer and can think more clearly, you remind yourself that your partner is not responsible for your stress at work and they didn't know their comment would hit so hard. You don't expect them to profusely apologize for the comment and admit fault, because you recognize that nobody is "right" in this situation. You choose to explain your feelings and ask them for a hug. Then you settle into your night together, focusing on relaxing and getting into a better emotional state.

As you read through this scenario, could you feel how tempting it is to jump to anger? We all feel hurt, disrespected, ignored, or de-prioritized by our partners sometimes, and even small events such as a comment about shoes can trigger big feelings. But, instead of an immediate reaction, pausing before responding allows us to self-reflect on why we're upset, self-soothe, and then choose an effective way of responding. The following client activities can introduce effective strategies for clients to begin self-soothing on their own.

Client Activity

Self-Soothing Strategies

When you're upset in a conversation, it's important to know how you can calm your body and regulate your emotions. Different strategies work for different people, but below are some of the most effective ways to return to your emotional baseline. Place a check mark on all the strategies you know work for you, and circle the ones you'd like to try in the future:

- ☐ Take a walk or spend some time in nature
- ☐ Exercise (e.g., yoga, running, strength training, walking, biking)
- ☐ Do a craft you enjoy, like knitting or scrapbooking
- ☐ Read a book or watch a show
- ☐ Listen to music
- ☐ Take a shower or bath
- ☐ Spend time walking or snuggling with your pet
- ☐ Journal your thoughts and feelings
- ☐ Meditate or do some deep breathing exercises
- ☐ Talk to a friend or family member
- ☐ Use a coloring book or mandala
- ☐ Take a nap
- ☐ Do a grounding exercise with each of your five senses (e.g., focus on a single item in the room, light a candle and focus on its scent)

Client Activity

Developing a Self-Soothing Plan

After checking off the strategies that would work best for you in *Self-Soothing Strategies*, use the space below to create an action plan for when you need to regulate your emotions. Since different conflict situations have different constraints and levels of intensity, we've organized the chart into categories to help you choose the best strategy for a given situation. For example, maybe you'd read a book if you were feeling irritated with your partner after a tough conversation, but you would need to talk with a friend or go for a run if you were feeling very angry or hurt after a fight. This is your action plan for returning to your emotional baseline the next time you feel emotionally flooded.

My Self-Soothing Plan

Activities for When I Am Only a Little Upset	Activities for When I Am at My Most Upset
Activities for When I Have a Little Time	**Activities for When I Have a Lot of Time**

Taking a Break

When you're able to identify dysregulation in your clients as it's happening, you give them an opportunity to calm their bodies before they reach a full-on flooded state. If you can sense building tension or anxiety during a session, pause the conversation and check in with your clients. How are they feeling in this moment? Is their heart rate increasing? Would they benefit from a pause to do a deep breathing exercise or grab a glass of cold water? Sometimes quick self-soothing strategies can lower the emotional "temperature" enough to continue a productive session.

However, you and your clients may not always realize when emotions are heating up, and quick interventions won't do enough to reregulate your clients. When your clients recognize they are emotionally flooded, they will likely need a break from the conversation. Remember, they won't be able to listen or communicate as effectively if they are in fight-or-flight mode.

Despite feeling flooded, many people, particularly pursuers or those with anxious attachments, will want to keep talking until the problem is resolved and they feel reconnected. However, pushing the issue when one or all partners are dysregulated will probably cause more damage in the relationship. When people are flooded, they are more likely to say things they regret and act in more extreme ways to be heard or feel protected. This is why it's essential to teach your clients not only how to recognize that they're feeling flooded but also how to get the time and space they need to recover their emotional baseline.

How to Ask for a Break

It's important that your clients know how to properly ask for a break during a conflict. Storming out of the room, stonewalling, or threatening a breakup are not effective or responsible ways of voicing their need for some time away from the conversation. These ways of exiting conflict will only increase the other person's anxiety, anger, and insecurity, making the conflict worse and making repair even more challenging.

When your clients need a break, they should first explain to their partner that they are feeling flooded. They can share details if they want. For instance, they could say, "Right now I can tell my anxiety is through the roof, and I'm not able to engage as effectively in our conversation." Being explicit about their emotional experience will help their partner have empathy and see that they aren't just avoiding the issue or withdrawing.

Next, your clients should voice what they need. This can be as simple as, "I need twenty minutes to myself," or it can provide more detail, such as, "I need at least two hours so I can think through everything and recenter myself." If they're going to leave the space or change a shared plan for the day, especially if it's for an extended period of time, they should explain that as well: "I need to get out of the house for a while. I'll be going for a run, but I'll be back in time for us to go to dinner." Clarifying in this way isn't done because they have to justify their needs or answer to their partner; it's done because it shows respect and maintains openness even during conflict.

Finally, healthy breaks must have an end point. Important conversations can't be dropped indefinitely when someone becomes dysregulated. While those with avoidant attachment or those who play the withdrawer role might prefer to end an argument and not come back to it, that will only make their partner anxious and untrusting. Your clients don't need to know the exact amount of time they'll need to recover emotionally, but they should give a timeframe for when they'll be ready to talk again. It can be specific ("Let's try talking about this again tonight after I've had time to think") or less certain but with more reassurance ("I don't know when I'll feel ready to talk about this, but I really want to work it out and I promise we'll come back to it.").

For couples who are unable to resume tough conversations with a more positive, productive approach, it may be most helpful to table conflicts until session, where they can have your support in working through the issue in a healthier way. Be sure to encourage clients to take breaks when you see them becoming flooded in session and to reinforce when they take responsible breaks outside of sessions.

How to Use Breaks Effectively

Once your clients know how to ask for breaks, they need to know what to do during their break and, perhaps more importantly, what *not* to do. Unfortunately, most people don't use breaks effectively and end up engaging in thoughts and behaviors that will make the conflict worse instead of better. A successful break will regulate your clients' emotions and prepare them to have a healthier, more effective conversation.

As tempting as it is for all of us, your clients should not use breaks to reinforce their perspective and "build their case." You've probably experienced this yourself—for example, you take a shower to cool down and find yourself thinking through how you would "win" an argument with someone. If your clients use a break to fortify their arguments and poke holes in their partner's perspective, it practically guarantees that the next fight will be much worse than the initial one.

Instead, encourage your clients to see breaks as having two purposes: First, clients should regulate their emotions using self-soothing strategies, as you read in the previous section. Second, they should try to see their partner's perspective. In the heat of a conflict, it's very hard to consider the other person's point of view, but with time and space, your clients can and should focus on understanding their partner's feelings and perspective. Remind them that they don't have to agree or give up their own point of view, but they do need to be open to their partner's take on the situation.

A break is successful when clients are emotionally regulated and can re-enter the conversation by saying, "I see your point, it makes sense to me why you're upset, and I want to talk about it." Starting the conversation with calmness and understanding will lower defenses. Everyone becomes more willing to listen, even in a difficult conversation, when they feel seen and heard by their partner from the start.

Coregulation

Coregulation is the ability to regulate our emotions and, in doing so, help our partner regulate their emotions as well. It means we can hear and tolerate our partner's feelings, helping them sort through difficult emotions and get back to their emotional baseline without needing to control, change, or fix these feelings. The ability to coregulate relies on the belief that our partner is trustworthy and won't leave us, and that we can have separate and even conflicting thoughts or feelings without risking the relationship. Partners in this type of relationship are comfortable with the other person having needs, thoughts, and feelings that are negative, challenging, or in conflict with their own. They can tolerate hearing difficult emotions or information without becoming angry, scared, or defensive.

Coregulation is a hallmark attribute of secure attachment. As you know from chapter 3, people with a secure attachment are committed, deeply value their partner, feel safe voicing their feelings or needs in the relationship, and feel comfortable hearing their partner's feelings and needs. People with secure attachments care for their partner but know that the relationship is just one component of their life, and they do not let the relationship status dictate everything. For example, if their partner is upset with them, the person can still function at work instead of being completely consumed with distress or emotionally detaching from the relationship. They know that they have other meaningful relationships with family or friends, that they have other duties or goals outside of their partnership, and that they will be okay even during tough times with their partner or if the relationship ends.

As you can tell, coregulation requires self-awareness and strong emotion regulation skills. Clients who quickly become dysregulated and consumed by their own emotions will not be able to help their partners regulate. Indeed, some clients will complain about this, saying that every time they get upset, they end up comforting their partner instead of getting comfort themselves. When clients are intensely influenced by their partner's feelings or, on the other side, unaffected by their partner, they need to work on their emotional boundaries.

Emotional boundaries are the invisible line between partners' emotional experiences and perspectives. By differentiating one person's thoughts and feelings from their partner's, emotional boundaries help partners self-regulate and maintain respect in their relationship. In healthy relationships, emotional boundaries are:

- **Clear:** Partners communicate if their boundaries are crossed so the other knows a behavior has been hurtful.
- **Consistent:** Partners can expect the same standard of behavior and response.
- **Flexible:** Partners recognize that situations will sometimes require different responses, and that a one-size-fits-all approach to conflict will miss the nuance that romantic relationships require.

There are two kinds of emotional boundaries that are necessary for coregulation: the external and the internal. The *external emotional boundary* is like an invisible force field that surrounds an individual, filtering the words or feelings that come in and stopping certain things from making them feel bad, such as unreasonable claims about their personality or cruel comments about their behavior. The external boundary should let some things through so they can be reflective on their areas of growth as a person and in a relationship, but it needs to be selective about what it allows to get through. People can make unkind or untrue claims when they are heated and upset, and your clients need to have a strong enough sense of self to weed out statements that don't seem accurate.

The *internal emotional boundary* is like a force field inside an individual that filters the words and feelings that they let out. This boundary is the net that stops them from saying overly harsh things about their partner that they don't truly believe or should express more compassionately. It catches and contains your clients' painful feelings so that they don't vent their anger, anxiety, or frustration onto others in ways they will regret.

Many clients need to fortify or soften these boundaries. For example, clients with an overly solid external emotional boundary will not be able to take in important feedback about how their actions impact others. If their external boundary is too weak, they will believe everything their partner says about them and will become emotionally dysregulated and overwhelmed by their partner's judgments or opinions.

Having no emotional boundaries in a relationship is known as *enmeshment*. In enmeshed relationships, partners are too intertwined and are unable to separate their feelings from one another. What one partner feels, the other does as well. There is often a lack of respect for each other's boundaries, such as insisting that a topic be discussed even if one partner feels too drained or upset to talk about it. This can lead to *codependency*, where one partner is fully reliant on the other to meet all their emotional needs.

In contrast, emotional boundaries that are too rigid create emotional distance in a relationship. In this type of relationship, your clients probably don't share their feelings with each other and resist engaging in emotionally intense conversations in order to avoid heightened feelings. Explaining the concept of emotional boundaries to your clients will allow them to assess their own boundaries and determine what boundaries they need to improve.

A good analogy to use with your clients is that they each have their own emotional thermostat. This thermostat allows them to be in control of their own emotional temperature, no matter what's happening outside of them. If it's too "warm," they can turn the thermostat down to stay cool. If it's "icy," they know how to warm themselves up. Ideally, your clients will develop strong thermostats that stay true to their set temperature instead of responding to the outside climate.

However, your clients should know that the way they were parented can impact their internal thermostat. For example, parents who shamed their child for feeling upset might teach them to block out the world around them (i.e., not let anything or anyone change their temperature); this client can end up developing overly rigid external emotional boundaries and present as unaffected, unyielding, avoidant, or angry.

Further, as couples get closer, they may slowly lose their independent thermostats and start sharing one relationship thermostat. No longer do they have separate zones in their household. Instead, one thermostat is in charge of the entire space. If one person gets heated, so does the other. If one person goes icy cold, their partner does the same. Instead of setting their own temperature, their internal thermostats match the external climate.

Now, even two people with exceptionally good emotional thermostats will change temperature during conflict. During arguments, some people run hot (i.e., yelling), some people run cold (i.e., stonewalling), and yes, some stay in that sweet spot of 70 degrees. Your clients need to learn that if their partner gets down to 30 degrees in a fight or shoots up to 95 degrees, they can take a deep breath and stay in control of their own thermostat. They can observe their partner's feelings, but they don't have to let anyone else's temperature change their own. If they do become upset by their partner's mood, they can practice self-soothing strategies to return to their emotional baseline. The calmer person in the room, or the one who has the stronger emotion-regulation skills, should lead the way in maintaining their temperature despite the changing emotional climate.

By helping your clients learn emotion regulation skills, you'll enable them to learn how to engage in coregulation as well. This is particularly important because being able to coregulate helps couples feel connected, secure, and loved, even during conflict. In the next chapter, you'll learn how conflict affects romantic relationships, what people do that makes conflicts worse, and how your clients can better manage conflicts together.

Client Activity

Emotional Boundaries

This exercise will allow you to take some time to reflect on your own emotional boundaries. You can share responses with your partner if you find it helpful or bring your responses into session to discuss with your therapist. Place a check mark next to the things you tend to do when you're fighting with your partner.

During an argument or disagreement, do you . . .

- ☐ Say everything you think, even if it's very hurtful
- ☐ Swear at your partner, raise your voice, or use sarcasm
- ☐ Formulate criticisms based on your partner's insecurities or flaws they've admitted to in the past
- ☐ Stonewall or refuse to speak altogether
- ☐ Feel that everything your partner says is an attack on your character
- ☐ Withdraw emotionally or try to escape the conversation by ignoring your partner or leaving the room
- ☐ Agree with all your partner's points and feel terrible about yourself
- ☐ Think that none of your partner's points are valid and refuse to consider their perspective

If you checked off some or all of the first four boxes, your internal boundary probably needs some work. If you checked off some or all of the last four boxes, you may need to review your external boundaries. Remember that boundaries can be either too weak or too rigid, and partners in healthy relationships have boundaries that require balance and collaboration.

After discovering more about your emotional boundaries, reflect on the following questions.

Which boundary (internal or external) is best established for you? Which one could use work? Are they both too strong or too weak?

____

____

____

How have previous relationships and life experiences impacted your emotional boundaries?

____

____

____

How has a weak or overly fortified boundary negatively impacted you? How has it impacted your partner? How has it complicated your communication, especially in arguments?

____

____

____

What about your partner's boundaries—do you see them as too strong, too weak, or just right? How do their boundaries interact with your boundaries during conflicts?

____

____

____

CHAPTER 5

Managing Conflict

Now that your clients have an understanding of their attachment style, know their role in the negative cycle, can identify feeling flooded, and are comfortable engaging in self-soothing strategies to regulate their emotions, we are going to look more closely at what many couples say is the most difficult and upsetting part of their relationship: conflict. Arguing with a partner can be distressing, confusing, and even scary, but it doesn't have to be. Conflict simply means there is a mismatch in your clients' needs, feelings, or opinions. Discovering this mismatch is actually an opportunity for them to better understand each other and strengthen their relationship through compassion and compromise. However, as we know from chapter 3, your clients are likely stuck in a negative cycle that is preventing them from taking advantage of this opportunity. By better understanding common mistakes people make during arguments (and what to do instead), you can guide your clients in communicating more effectively during conflict.

This chapter is focused on specific behaviors that worsen conflict and how you can help your clients recognize and change these behaviors. As you address behaviors, remember to validate your clients' feelings—you don't want to make them feel ashamed of how they've acted. Remember that their behaviors, even if extreme, have been attempts to be heard by their partner or feel safe and protected from painful feelings during arguments. Help them hold self-compassion alongside the desire to change.

Foundational Information on Conflict

While most couples would love to have a conflict-free relationship, it's simply not realistic or possible. Relationships are constantly going through a cycle of harmony, rupture, and repair. Clients should know that disagreements and disconnection will happen and, rather than seeking to eliminate conflict completely, make it their goal to intentionally come together after such conflicts occur, seek to understand and reconnect with each other, and return to a state of harmony.

Despite the inevitable fact that we all get into fights with our loved ones, we are never formally taught critical information about managing conflict in relationships. Having this information can make conflict less scary and give your clients the knowledge of how to navigate it effectively.

Key Aspects of Conflict

As mentioned in chapter 4, most conflicts in relationships are perpetual and not solvable (Gottman & Silver, 2015). Couples in very happy long-term relationships have the same arguments repeatedly without any resolution. The details of the argument may change over time, but the general issue remains the same. Your clients do *not* need to solve every problem that comes up in their relationship, and they shouldn't try to because it's not possible. They *do* need to learn how to talk about recurring issues in a way that makes them feel heard and respected.

Conflict is difficult because it causes attachment distress. Disagreeing threatens people's sense of security in their relationships because it often includes feeling unheard, uncared for, blamed, or rejected. People's reactions during conflict have less to do with the actual issue at hand, and more to do with the painful feelings that are rustled up by disagreeing with their partner. Most couples try to solve the problem without addressing the need to feel heard and connected, and in doing so, they can often make the conflict worse.

Avoiding conflict does not equal a better relationship and, in fact, can lead to resentment. It's important for you and your clients to know that learning to share their thoughts or make requests may lead to increased conflict at first, since this will be a real change in the dynamic, and that's okay. People in a relationship will not always agree with one another.

If clients are incredibly upset (i.e., *flooded*), they need to take a break from the conflict because they will no longer be able to effectively listen or communicate (Gottman & Silver, 2015). This step is absolutely critical—there is no point in continuing a conversation if either partner is flooded. They will not be able to listen or communicate as effectively, and the discussion is likely to escalate into a bigger issue and make them feel even more upset or confused. If that fight-or-flight response has been triggered, it's time for a break and some self-soothing.

In a conflict, your clients' primary goal should be listening to and understanding their partner. This runs counter to the idea that many people have: conflicts are a win-lose scenario. Many people feel that if they don't fight for their point and get an apology, they "lose" the argument. However, the real victory in a relational conflict is not that each person gets labeled as "right" or "wrong," but rather, that *all* people feel they were heard, respected, and understood.

Therapist Reference

Key Aspects of Conflict

- According to research by the Gottman Institute, 69 percent of conflicts that couples have are perpetual and not solvable.
- The goal is not to "solve" conflicts, but rather to have strong communication while navigating the issue.
- Conflict can be good! It allows people to share their hurts, needs, and boundaries. This can be hard, but being in a long-term relationship requires hard conversations.
- Absence of conflict does not mean a healthy relationship; avoiding issues can lead to resentment and unhappiness.
- People should take breaks from a conflict when they are emotionally flooded. (A break should last at least 15 minutes, but probably longer.)
- Conflicts can trigger attachment distress; people are often more upset by the painful feelings that the conflict brings up (e.g., they're not enough, their partner doesn't care about them) than by the specific problem being discussed.
- The goal in a conflict is not to "win." A win-lose, right-wrong mindset will only lead to escalating conflict. The goal is to both listen and be heard.

Common Mistakes During Conflict

There are some common mistakes that people make during conflicts that make things worse (sometimes *much* worse) instead of better. These can be learned behaviors, such as things that your clients observed their parents do when they argued, or they can be defense mechanisms, which are ways to protect them from feeling vulnerable or hurt. None of us are our most calm, rational, or kind selves during arguments; in fact, we are often much pettier, meaner, and unforgiving than our usual nature. We also tend to see the worst version of our partner during conflicts, only focusing on their perceived bad traits and unreasonableness during the discussion, which makes us feel more justified in being harsh or unrelenting.

Learning about the frequent errors people make in conflict is critical to helping your clients identify the mistakes they make. Self-awareness is the first ingredient necessary for growth and change. However, remember that you must also be sensitive to not shame your clients for engaging in these behaviors. Be compassionate as you explore where they may be making a misstep, providing reassurance that many people engage in similar behaviors and that they are usually protective in nature (even if they are not productive). This is not about finding blame for the problem, but rather helping each client see their role in contributing to the relationship's problems so they understand how they can change it for the better.

Some of these may sound obvious to your clients, and some will be able to quickly identity which errors they are prone to during conflict. However, other clients may not realize that these are even "mistakes" or see that they are engaging in these behaviors. For example, many people don't realize they are being defensive during conflict; they see their explanations as attempts to clarify their partner's misperceptions. It can be helpful to gently point out these behaviors during session, helping clients see examples of when they are engaging in a behavior that needs to change.

Defensiveness

Most people default to defensiveness during a conflict when they feel they are being accused, blamed, or attacked. Defensiveness is when people defend their actions or feelings by explaining why they were justified, and it is often followed by pointing out a similar or complementary flaw in their partner to show their partner's hypocrisy and shift the blame. As you may recall, this is one of Gottman's Four Horsemen, which means it is a predictor of divorce (Gottman & Silver, 2015).

Defensiveness is one of the most common responses in a conflict (or even conversation). Although subtle, defensiveness is quite destructive. When a person shares a feeling or need and is met with why they shouldn't feel or need that, it's invalidating and painful. The defensive partner tries to explain why they didn't do anything wrong (as a way to cope with their own painful feelings of guilt, fear, etc.), but it comes across as uncaring. It makes the first person feel they need to explain themselves in bigger, louder ways in order to be heard.

Stonewalling and Withdrawing

Stonewalling is when clients turn silent, feel numb, refuse to answer or engage in the conversation, or leave the discussion or room without saying a word. This happens when a person becomes overwhelmed during a conflict and emotionally shuts down. Stonewalling is another predictor of divorce (Gottman & Silver, 2015). Although it's understandable that a client may shut down, disengaging in this way can be damaging for the relationship. Their partner doesn't know what's happening, how to reach out, and when (or if) they will reengage in the conversation. Often, stonewalling ends conversations that don't get picked up later, which makes the other partner fear that they can't bring up hard topics and that their feelings and needs won't be addressed.

In the more extreme examples, stonewalling can go on for days, weeks, or months. In more abusive relationships, the partner seeking control will withhold communication or attention to punish their partner. Partners who stonewall for this length of time aren't doing it because they're overwhelmed by their feelings (self-soothing and returning to an emotional baseline can happen within hours), but rather to exert control in the relationship and send a message about what will happen if their partner does or says something they don't like.

Unregulated Anger

The opposite of stonewalling is when people express their anger and hurt without any modulation. In RLT this is considered one of the "Five Losing Strategies" and is described as "unbridled self-expression," when a partner says exactly how they feel without moderating their words or nonverbal communication (Real, 2008). It can also present as contempt, another strong predictor of divorce (Gottman & Silver, 2015). Unregulated anger can look like yelling, cruel assumptions and accusations, an unwillingness to de-escalate, and even violence, such as punching walls or throwing things. Unregulated anger quickly makes arguments worse because the person isn't interested in connecting over the issue and finding some sort of resolution. In this situation, the person is hurt and angry and wants to make sure their partner knows it.

In its worst form, unregulated anger is abusive. It's a partner screaming, blaming, and lobbing harsh judgments at their partner with no ability to regulate their behavior in the moment. These partners will hopefully come to their own conclusion—after the fight—about how damaging their behavior was, but some may need gentle help from a couples therapist to see that while their *feelings* are valid and justified, how they express the feelings is *not*.

Expanding the Problem

Arguments become more unmanageable when clients start bringing up past issues or globalizing the current issue at hand. In doing so, letting the conflict get bigger is a defensive response to deflect blame and avoid feeling badly in the current conversation. It makes sense as a way to shift the conversation and lessen those feelings, but unfortunately, it makes the conflict worse and harder to repair. This also leads to scorekeeping, which is never helpful for relationships. When your clients are recalling all the ways the other has hurt them in the past and tallying up who has been more hurt, it's time to interrupt the conversation. Scorekeeping is ineffective because each partner inevitably thinks *they* are the more wronged partner, and dredging up old wounds can make all involved feel increasingly frustrated, indignant, and unwilling to repair.

Viewing the Other Entirely Negatively

Conflicts bring up difficult feelings and often lead to people not behaving their best, which makes it easy to see one's partner negatively. This happens during negative sentiment override, when partners see everything the other person says or does in a negative light (Gottman & Silver, 2015). In RLT, this overly negative image that leaves out any positive attributes (Real, 2008) is called the *core negative image* (CNI). Similar to Gottman's negative sentiment override, when someone is seeing the CNI version of their partner, they take everything the partner says or does in a negative and unforgiving way. Further, when clients begin to see their partner as *wholly* bad, it will be difficult to have a productive conversation.

Failed Repair Attempts

Repair attempts are any gesture meant to de-escalate the conflict, reduce negativity, and reconnect. It can be physical touch, an apology, or even a kind joke to lighten the mood. Repair attempts are extensions of love, care, and connection when things are feeling hard. A missed or rejected repair attempt can feel very painful to the person who extended it. It's a vulnerable act to extend an olive branch, so to speak, by trying to lower the intensity and reconnect. When partners ignore or outright reject a repair attempt, it often escalates the situation further and makes the person even less likely to try to make things better again.

Repair attempts fail either when one partner does not see the other partner or chooses not to accept them. More often than not, partners do not recognize a repair attempt has been made. They overlook the soft expression of understanding from their partner, the hand reaching out to touch their arm, or the little joke to calm them down. They blow past these moments that could have been connecting. Some people even take repair attempts as indicators that because their partner is calm and showing love, they can share their frustration even more emphatically, which escalates the conflict. At other times, people do see the repair attempts for what it is but are too angry to accept it. They see the other person reaching out to connect but feel too hurt to do that. Or, if they're really angry, they see it as an opportunity to reject the effort and make their partner hurt as much as they do.

Needing to be Right

Humans love to be right. Even if we're right about something bad, we like knowing that our thoughts, intuitions, or feelings were true. However, this desire for rightness is usually not helpful in relationships because people have different perspectives and realities; fundamentally, no one is ever fully "right." Many clients will struggle with this concept because they have been hardwired to believe that there is one reality and someone has to be right. They may even think that arguments can only be resolved by figuring out who was right. Couples that battle over who is right are destined to feel invalidated, unheard, and frustrated, as it's rare for someone to concede that their perspective or feelings are outright "wrong." Instead, the more someone fights to be right, the more their partner will dig in their heels about their own perspective.

This is where you'll see clients getting stuck in the content of their arguments. They debate what each person actually said, or disagree about the tone used or the order in which they said things; this type of minutiae-focused conversation isn't productive. They will probably never agree on who said what or how the issue unfolded, and the energy they're spending on reconciling their different perspectives is leading to frustration and disconnection. Further, their efforts to convince their partner that they are right will make their partner dig in their heels even further, making them feel more stuck. The old saying of "You can be right or you can be married" originally had a different intention behind it, but it's actually true. If your clients can't let go of needing to be right, they'll be unhappy and eventually alone. Clients need to move from needing to be right to needing to be heard.

Verbal Abuse

Many people do not realize that they are engaging in verbal abuse, in part because these behaviors have become normalized on television. Verbal abuse includes being sarcastic, swearing, imitating or mocking, screaming, attacking someone's character, name-calling, making cruel jokes, or making threats. When people become emotionally dysregulated, they may escalate their behaviors in their attempts to stop the conversation or to hurt their partner just as they feel hurt, and that can result in verbal abuse. Verbal abuse is unacceptable and is a line that shouldn't be crossed, as it only serves to deepen the pain and disconnection.

Remember from chapter 1 that evidence of verbal abuse during fights does not necessarily mean a relationship is abusive. This is because many people have done some of these unacceptable things during fights in their desperation to be heard or to stop the conversation, only to later regret using these tactics. For example, some clients will recognize that screaming or swearing is problematic and want help to learn new ways of interacting. They will be a good fit for couples therapy. Clients who don't see a problem with these behaviors and think their partner is the one who needs fixing are likely not a good fit.

Gaslighting

Gaslighting falls under the category of verbal abuse, but it deserves its own category because it is commonly misunderstood. Gaslighting is not simply disagreeing or telling someone they are wrong; it's when someone attempts to thoroughly convince their partner that they're "crazy" for thinking the way they do. If a person is attempting to control how their partner thinks or feels about a situation or trying to persuade them that they are wrong about their beliefs by making them doubt their judgment or reality, this is gaslighting.

This is very different from the normal disagreements couples have about "who's right." Many people try to persuade their partner that they are right about a feeling, memory, or perspective, but it's not in effort to gain control or power in the relationship. Needing to be right and disagreeing on the facts, although not productive, is not abusive. It is a human instinct to preserve the validity of our experience by having our partner agree with us, whereas gaslighting is a control tactic used in an abusive relationship. To help differentiate the two, recall that abusive behaviors are part of a cycle; that is, gaslighting typically occurs alongside other abusive behaviors as one partner tries to control or manipulate the other.

Overly Strong or Weak Emotional Boundaries

As you'll recall from chapter 4, there are two important emotional boundaries to understand: internal and external. The internal emotional boundary is what contains and filters your clients' thoughts and feelings. If it's not too strong and not too weak, this boundary lets them speak their mind in a way that is accurate and appropriate. The external emotional boundary protects them from outside information. When this boundary is working at its best, they can consider others' thoughts and feelings without either automatically dismissing them or assuming they are correct. When these two boundaries are at a healthy place, your clients can give and take information without becoming dysregulated (e.g., overly angry, sad, overwhelmed), even during a disagreement.

Poor Internal Emotional Boundary

If a client's internal boundary is weak, they will say things without considering the impact it will have on others. They may say hurtful, mean things, perhaps things they don't actually believe, and they will likely say them in an overly harsh manner. "Firing every bullet in the gun" like this is dangerous. First of all, the client can apologize after the conflict, but they can never erase what they said, and if they say some truly harsh things, their partner is going to struggle to forgive and forget. Second, this action escalates the conflict very quickly and unproductively. Third, the client's points or feelings are effectively discredited once their harshness becomes the issue. They do themselves a disservice by becoming mean and hurtful, since they *do* have valid feelings and important needs to communicate, but it gets overshadowed when their way of sharing it becomes problematic or, at the extreme, verbally abusive. People with weak internal emotional boundaries tend to be the pursuers in relationships, insisting on a "resolution" to the conflict to the detriment of the relationship.

When a client's internal boundary is too strong, they tend to filter what they say too much and might not even say anything at all for fear of how it will impact their partner. They're likely to conceal how they really think and feel, stonewall, or withdraw entirely from the conversation, which isn't productive. People with overly fortified internal emotional boundaries are often withdrawers in the relationship, fearing that anything they say will make things worse or somehow be "wrong."

Poor External Emotional Boundary

A client who has a weak external boundary lets everything affect them. They have no filter protecting them from their partner's feelings or complaints. If their partner makes a comment about their messiness, for example, they feel instantly hurt and attacked, instead of taking time to consider if their complaint is valid ("*Am* I messy?") or if their partner is actually stressed about something else and taking it out on the one empty glass they left on the countertop. These clients need to learn how to not let every comment or feeling cut to their core and make them upset. Not everything their partner says about them is right or true, and only they get to decide what is accurate.

In contrast, an external boundary that's too strong means that a client won't consider anything their partner is saying and is likely to act defensively or dismissively. Clients who disregard their partner's feedback are unwilling to be self-reflective and consider the possibility that they have erred or could grow in certain ways. Although you don't want your clients to take everything their partners say as automatically correct, you (and their partner) do want them to give their partner's perspective some consideration.

Not Taking a Break

When clients become flooded, they will have a hard time engaging productively in the conversation. They may cry uncontrollably, become angry and impossible to talk to, shut down, or panic. Again, these feelings are understandable, but this type of emotional dysregulation will make it very difficult to have hard conversations and reach a place of understanding and repair. While your clients can't control if they become flooded, they can control what to do when it happens. Staying in the conflict when they are not capable of effectively listening or communicating won't help. Similarly, not allowing an emotionally flooded partner to take a break and instead pushing them to keep talking (or even following them when they try to remove themselves from the situation) will also make the conflict worse.

The Outcome of These Mistakes

Whether your clients are yelling regretful things or stonewalling their partner during fights, the impact is the same: these mistakes damage relationships by escalating conflict and weakening secure attachments.

They make people dread challenging conversations, and their anticipation of the worst possibly outcome often becomes a self-fulfilling prophecy.

Some mistakes do more damage than others (e.g., verbal abuse is more destructive than needing to be right), but over time all these mistakes add up to harm in the relationship. Most importantly, failing to show accountability afterward and repair these mistakes erodes the stability of the relationship. Partners can't count on each other to navigate fights. They feel attacked, unheard, and alone. They leave these conversations feeling worse about the relationship than they did about the original issue. Help your clients to identify their conflict mistakes with the following activity. With recognition comes the ability to improve.

Client Activity

Identifying Your Conflict Mistakes

Look over the following list of common mistakes people make in conflicts and place a check mark next to the mistakes you tend to make. Write down some examples if you can. If you're currently single, think back over all your past relationships and look for patterns of what conflict mistakes you most often make with your partners. Also look for any patterns in the types of mistakes your partners make—this will tell you something about the type of partners you're choosing.

- ☐ Defensiveness: ______________________________
- ☐ Stonewalling and withdrawing: ______________________________
- ☐ Unregulated anger: ______________________________
- ☐ Expanding the problem: ______________________________
- ☐ Viewing the other person entirely negatively: ______________________________
- ☐ Failed repair attempts: ______________________________
- ☐ Needing to be right: ______________________________
- ☐ Verbal abuse:
  - ☐ Yelling or screaming: ______________________________
  - ☐ Swearing or name-calling: ______________________________
  - ☐ Mocking or mimicking: ______________________________
  - ☐ Cruel sarcasm: ______________________________
  - ☐ Harsh blaming or denigrating: ______________________________
- ☐ Gaslighting: ______________________________
- ☐ Poor internal emotional boundary:

- ☐ Weak internal boundary: ______________________________
- ☐ Overly fortified internal boundary: ______________________________

☐ Poor external emotional boundary:

- ☐ Weak external boundary: ______________________________
- ☐ Overly fortified external boundary: ______________________________

☐ Not taking a break or not allowing partner to take a break: ______________

If you're currently in a relationship and you and your partner can discuss these subjects without anger or judgment, try sitting down together and brainstorming what each of you do during fights. Look at patterns in your arguments and where you often get stuck. What stops you from seeing the other perspective, finding a resolution, or moving on?

Strategies for Managing Conflict

Conflict may look different in different relationships, but when people have close relationships with others for a long enough time, they will eventually have conflict. It's inevitable. That's why the goal of couples work isn't to avoid or prevent conflict, but to initiate and navigate it more effectively. This section will look at more productive and healthier ways that your clients can manage conflict or hard conversations.

Many of these strategies are the opposite of the common mistakes you learned about earlier. For example, instead of speaking harshly with unregulated anger, couples should always communicate with respect. You'll also find additional evidence-based recommendations for helping couples navigate healthy conflict, such as starting conversations with love and gentleness.

Couples often come to therapy wanting tools and strategies for better communication. You can certainly start teaching them the skills in this section early on, but it will be most effective to have them first understand their negative cycle and how their actions contribute to the problems at hand. Some couples do well with concrete lists of what they need to do (and not do) in order to have a better relationship—the following skills are what they're looking for (along with emotional regulation skills from chapter 4).

Start Gently

How we start difficult conversations sets the tone for the rest of the discussion. In general, people initiate and pursue conversations in an overly harsh manner that makes their partner defensive, hurt, and angry. In contrast, showing love and care even as a difficult subject is broached helps maintain closeness and a sense of security. The Gottman Institute calls this strategy a "gentle start-up" or "soft start-up"—specifically, they describe it as a partner initiating a conversation with kindness and respect, focusing on their own experience, refraining from blame, and expressing what they need in positive terms (Gottman & Silver, 2015).

For example, your clients can begin by sharing something kind or loving about their partner, which will make their partner feel secure in the relationship and thus more likely to listen nondefensively to what they have to say. They should open the conversation in a gentle manner, maintaining calmness and politeness as they explain their feelings without blaming or accusing their partner. Also, they should express understanding and appreciation throughout the conversation to continue establishing love and security. To make a gentle start-up easier, your clients shouldn't wait until they're bursting with frustration, or they'll probably speak harshly and without much context. They need to speak up at the first sign of an issue.

Offer Validation

Validation is when a client sees their partner's side and understands where they are coming from. It makes their partner feel heard, seen, and safe. Validation means saying, "I understand why you feel that way, it makes total sense, and I'm glad you told me." Now, people often struggle with this because they incorrectly believe that validation equals agreement. It does not. Your clients don't have to agree with their partner or think that they're right to offer validation; they simply need to voice understanding and respect for their partner's perspective and feelings.

Instead of becoming defensive, trying to control their partner's feelings, gaslighting them into seeing things their own way, or taking any other negative strategy to fight for how they feel, your clients need to embrace their partner's perspective and feelings as valid. Remind your clients that just because they have a different perspective or experience, it doesn't make their partner's perspective invalid. They can work to verbalize how they understand their partner's point of view and validate how they feel.

Lower Your Defenses

Clients jump to defensiveness because they feel blamed or attacked. Some clients have an automatic defensive response because of an emotional wall that prevents them from really listening to and considering their partner's point of view. They can make it a goal to take a slow, deep breath and lower their defenses prior to a tough conversation. They need to hear what their partner is telling them without putting up a wall, deflecting blame, or justifying their actions. Tell them to listen as if they were listening to a friend talk about a relationship issue, trying to understand their side and take in how they feel. Encourage your clients to not jump to explaining why they acted a certain way or why their partner is wrong in how they feel, because that won't help. For the relationship to work, they need to be able to tell each other difficult things—even things that one person strongly disagrees with.

One way to take in the other person's perspective is to spend time asking clarifying questions and validating how they feel. Remember, validation doesn't equal agreement; a client can disagree with their partner's perspective and see things very differently while still acknowledging their partner's feelings and expressing that they understand their partner's point of view.

Don't Expand the Problem

As tempting as it may be to deflect blame and pull out the scorecard of hurts, your clients must learn to stay focused on the issue at hand. Expanding the problem does two things: First, it makes the conflict feel escalated and unmanageable. Clients get lost trying to keep track of the conversation and figure out what they're actually talking about. Second, it makes people hesitant to voice concerns in the future, fearing that it will lead to a huge conflict and that their original concern won't be addressed in the end.

Now, if the current conversation is bringing up feelings about past issues or new ones that need to be addressed, that's perfectly okay, but it shouldn't be added to the current discussion. Otherwise, a simple complaint can quickly spiral into a much bigger argument. Your clients should bring up the other concerns at another time—after the current issue has been resolved. Learning how to stay focused on the present problem and save other concerns for separate conversations will help your clients contain their arguments.

Stay Present Through Self-Soothing

Conflict is inherently dysregulating since it threatens the sense of peace and security in the relationship. Learning to stay present and calm in moments of disagreement or tension is critical for navigating conflict. In particular, it is the remedy for withdrawing and stonewalling, since people who engage in these behaviors are usually overwhelmed by their feelings and need to pull away to protect themselves. You can help your clients identify the signs that they're becoming flooded—using both physiological and emotional indicators. It's important that you teach them mindfulness and grounding skills (i.e., self-soothing strategies) to use during arguments and in session so they can build tolerance for painful feelings. Finally, you can help them ask for a break when they need it and teach them the most effective ways to use that time to reregulate and return to the conversation.

Be Curious and Create Dialogue

Your clients need to embrace the truth that conflicts are not about who is right or who is assigned blame. Going into a conversation with the belief that an argument can be "won," that one partner is right and needs to get the other to surrender, will prevent them from taking another perspective and engaging in a healthy dialogue.

Many clients will have a hard time letting go of the belief that in every fight, someone "wins" and someone "loses." However, this perspective will cause them to be argumentative, unyielding, and ultimately unsuccessful. You need to help your clients reframe the purpose of conflict. The goal is actually not to be right or even to solve the problem. Rather, the goal is to be curious about and gain understanding of the other's feelings and perspectives. During session, guide each of your clients to take turns sharing their experience and understanding of the problem while the other listens and validates. Help your clients let go of the need to be right by teaching them how to truly listen to their partner instead of constructing their counterpoint. A conversation or conflict is a success if all partners walk away with a greater understanding of each other's feelings and needs.

Maintain Respect

When people get emotionally dysregulated, their ability to communicate effectively plummets. Instead of speaking in a calm and clear manner, they use aggressive or intense language to show how hurt they are. This escalation can often lead to language that is exaggerated, harsh, or even cruel and abusive, all of which are very destructive for relationships. A core tenet of healthy communication is that no matter how mad someone gets, they still speak with respect. There is no excuse for being vicious to one's partner. You can teach your clients to use respectful language, keep their voice at a reasonable level, apologize if they overstep, and refrain from any of the verbal abuse, such as mocking or gaslighting. If a client is too upset to speak with respect, they need to take a break from the conversation.

See the Other Accurately

Instead of slipping into negative sentiment override (see chapter 3) or seeing the core negative image version of their partner, your clients will benefit from maintaining a more balanced and accurate view of each other. This will help them interact with more kindness and empathy. If you notice your clients slipping into an overly negative view of their partner, you can pause the conversation and help them shift mindsets from "me versus them" to "we're in this together." Help them remember that they chose this partner, and they have reasons why they care for this person. Support them in practicing empathy and taking their partner's perspective to help them see that, although they may disagree, their partner is not being completely unreasonable.

Extend and Accept Repair Attempts

Conflicts are de-escalated through repair attempts, which are any gesture (verbal or physical) meant to reduce the negativity of the conversation (Gottman & Silver, 2015). Strong couples are able to extend and accept repair attempts even when things are heated. These "olive branches" can be as simple as reaching out to touch the other person's hand as a gesture of connection and understanding, or they can be more in depth, such as a verbal validation of the other's perspective and voicing a desire to work together as a team in solving the issue. Repair attempts can also be jokes to lighten the mood (when appropriate), expressions of love and reassurance, offering physical touch, or apologies.

Just as important as learning how to extend repair attempts is learning how to accept them. Many people will ignore or outright reject their partner's repair attempts, which serves to escalate the tension even further, as their partner feels hurt and angry that their effort to reconnect is dismissed. Even if your clients do not feel ready to fully embrace their partner's repair, a sincere acknowledgment that their partner is trying to reduce the negativity can go a long way. It can be something as simple as "I see and appreciate that you're trying to lighten the mood and reconnect right now."

Work on Emotional Boundaries

An important part of staying emotionally regulated and open during conflict is having healthy emotional boundaries. People with strong but semi-permeable emotional boundaries are able to consider their partner's perspective without accepting every criticism as true, and they can share their thoughts and feelings in an appropriate and productive manner. In other words, they effectively filter what comes in and what comes out. When clients acknowledge and work on their emotional boundaries (see chapter 4), they are more likely to understand which boundaries need fortifying or softening.

Check In

Arguments can move quickly, and people may find out they are more upset than they realized at first. Pausing your clients during heightened conversations so they can check in with each other is a great way for them to de-escalate and reconnect. By stopping the content of the conversation and focusing instead on their feelings, they have an opportunity to show that they care about their partner feeling heard and safe. Prompt your clients to ask each other how they're feeling and to offer empathy and validation in response. They can also make sure they understand their partner by explaining how they think their partner feels and inviting feedback, letting their partner clarify or amend anything that they think wasn't quite right. During this pause, also encourage your clients to check in with themselves, assessing how they're feeling in the moment and what they may need.

Take Breaks

As you know, clients who are emotionally flooded need a break; it's not productive to continue the conversation at this point. However, a break doesn't mean shutting down or walking away from the conversation; those are stonewalling tactics, and they do more harm than good. An effective break requires communication—your clients need to say clearly that they're too upset to keep talking and need some time to reset. Breaks also require time limits. Clients can't just "pause" the conversation indefinitely—that would be avoidance. Teach your clients to initiate a break by first telling their partner that they're feeling flooded, then asking for a pause in the conversation so they can calm their bodies down, and finally, suggesting a time to resume. During the break, they should use self-soothing strategies to get back to their emotional baseline, such as exercising or meditating (a more comprehensive list is provided in chapter 4).

Client Activity

Strengthening Conflict Skills

Review the list of conflict skills below and consider what skills would be most beneficial for you, given what you already know about your attachment style, mistakes you commonly make during conflict, and your emotional needs and limits. Place a check mark next to the skills you already have and circle the ones you'd like to work on:

- ☐ Starting gently when bringing up concerns or requests
- ☐ Offering validation to your partner so they know you see and care about their feelings
- ☐ Lowering your defenses when your partner is sharing their feelings or needs
- ☐ Not expanding the problem into something bigger
- ☐ Staying present in the discussion by using self-soothing strategies if you get upset
- ☐ Being curious about your partner's thoughts and feelings and striving to create dialogue instead of focusing on being right or "winning"
- ☐ Keeping your language respectful at all times, even when you're furious
- ☐ Seeing your partner accurately rather than focusing on their flaws or seeing them as your enemy
- ☐ Extending and accepting repair attempts in order to reconnect
- ☐ Strengthening or softening your emotional boundaries so that you speak honestly but with kindness and take in what your partner says without becoming devastated or infuriated
- ☐ Checking in with how your partner is feeling during tough conversations
- ☐ Asking for breaks when you need them, and using those breaks productively

What Is a "Resolved" Conflict?

If your clients use the strategies from the last section, chances are they will have kinder, more productive conversations. They're more likely to understand their partner's feelings and needs and have theirs understood, too. But what does the "end" of a conflict look like?

Sometimes conflicts conclude with a full resolution, where the issue at hand is addressed, a concession or compromise is made, and a plan to prevent future similar mishaps is agreed upon. These are the types of endings that your clients will hope and strive for, and they may even expect therapy to teach them how to arrive at these types of gratifying conclusions every time there is a conflict.

However, endings sometimes look like agreeing to disagree. Your clients will struggle with this as being a "good" outcome, particularly those who have a "win-lose" mindset about arguments. But the truth is that they won't always get on the same page, even with the best communication. There are times when they won't agree with their partner's perspective even if they understand it, and that's okay. As mentioned before, research shows that the majority of conflicts in relationships (69 percent of them) are recurring and unsolvable, so the real goal of any conflict is to increase understanding and connection (Gottman & Silver, 2015). That's why every argument should be seen as an opportunity for the couple to know one another better and to practice self-regulation and coregulation. Issues can remain unresolved and the conflict can still be a success.

CHAPTER 6

Special Topics in Couples Work

Working with couples will *always* include improving communication, teaching conflict resolution skills, and strengthening their attachment. However, there are also more relationship-specific topics that you will face in your work; this chapter looks at a few of the more common ones.

First, we'll look at working with non-monogamous partnerships, meaning "couples" that include more than two people. This includes couples with open relationships or those in more structured polyamorous relationships. Next, you'll learn the key ingredients of working through infidelity. Then you will learn about the niche of discernment counseling, which is short-term work with couples to decide if they want to divorce. Finally, we'll explore how to identify and address issues of abuse.

Working with Non-monogamous Couples

Ethical non-monogamy (ENM) is when couples have an explicit and consensual agreement to have multiple romantic or sexual partnerships. ENM relationships require all partners to be informed and willingly consent to the relationship. This means they should have continuous open conversations about their needs and relationship boundaries. This is in contrast to how we understand *open relationships*: when two people decide to remove the boundaries of their current partnership so that they can develop emotional or sexual connections with other people. When people think of an open relationship, they often think of two people who are unsatisfied in some way and want to meet their needs by finding other temporary partners, but without having explicit conversations about the boundaries of their new arrangement. An open relationship without expectations, limits, and continuous communication is destined to cause hurt and harm. If you're working with clients considering a change to their relationship structure, encourage them to pursue an ENM relationship instead of a vague open relationship, as this will give them a better chance of finding satisfaction without hurting their original partnership.

There are many types of ENM relationship structures, so when working with non-monogamous couples, it is important to thoroughly understand what non-monogamy looks like for them specifically. There are an infinite number of ways to be non-monogamous, so you need to take the time to learn how your clients define their relationships. For example, how many people are involved? Are the other relationships mostly sexual, or are they romantic as well? Is there a hierarchy to their relationships? Do your clients know and interact with each other's partners? Don't make assumptions about your clients' relationship structures; let them define those structures for you.

Once you understand the structure of your clients' ENM relationship, you will need to balance the needs of their relationship with the needs of their outside relationships as well. In other words, working with ENM couples can be like working with multiple relationships at the same time, with the added complexity of having to balance the relationships with one another. Although your clients have agreed to cocreate an ENM relationship, each partner may have different feelings or concerns about it. Some are unequivocally enthusiastic, whereas others may be worried about various scenarios that have happened or could unfold. Your job in working with ENM couples is to create a safe space for them to process their feelings and concerns together, to avoid making assumptions about how non-monogamy impacts their relationship, and to show them that ENM relationships require continuous conversation and calibration as they evolve (Bairstow, 2017).

Many of the frameworks and interventions across couples therapy orientations apply to working with ENM couples. Although these relationships have more people involved and even more alliances to address, addressing attachment issues or wounds and strengthening communication and conflict management skills all still apply. Individuals in ENM relationships often (but not always) have advanced communication and emotion regulation skills, as they have had to speak openly about their needs in the process of cocreating their own relationship structure.

Common Issues in ENM Relationships

Stigma

Recent studies have estimated that about 4 to 5 percent of the population is in an ENM relationship (Levine et al., 2018). Although these relationship structures are slowly becoming more accepted, ENM relationships have always suffered from stigma. Most people are taught and internalize the myth that sexual exclusivity is the hallmark of a strong relationship, which results in many people making erroneous and harmful assumptions about ENM. Many assume that ENM couples are trying to fix their relationship by opening it up, or they don't actually want to be together but are too afraid of separating. It's also common to assume that ENM relationships are sexually promiscuous (with a negative connotation), dangerous (such as spreading sexually transmitted infections [STIs]) or an attempt to "have it all." (Moors, 2023). These misconceptions are not supported by research but have nevertheless constructed the dominant narrative about people who participate in ENM relationships; this narrative creates an environment where clients in ENM relationships may feel they have to hide the truth of their relationships. Therefore, effectively treating clients in ENM relationships requires identifying and challenging internalized beliefs or biases and gaining cultural competency.

A study asking polyamorous individuals to identify what challenges they face and what therapists should know when working with this population concluded that polyamorous individuals need support dealing with stigma and navigating their relationship; therefore, a couples therapist should feel comfortable addressing both of these concerns (Kisler & Lock, 2019). Understandably, your clients may worry that you have judgments and assumptions about their relationship. To counter this fear, you can proactively promote your acceptance of all relationship structures. You can share with them the trainings you've done to better understand ENM relationships and reassure them that although facing stigma is undoubtedly a frequent experience for them, it won't be a factor in their therapy with you.

However, you cannot help a couple deal with the stigma they face if *you* feel discomfort or judgment in response to their relationship. Working with this population may bring up unconscious thoughts or feelings that you need to become aware of and work through (see the *Identifying Biases* therapist reflection in chapter 1).

Negotiating the Relationship Structure

Many ENM couples will encounter difficulties in the process of cocreating their relationship. Deviating from the traditional monogamous setup requires self-work (such as knowing one's boundaries or emotional and sexual needs) in addition to couples work. Despite their desire to create a unique relationship structure, there will be disagreements and heightened emotions as they do so. Couples need to challenge the deeply ingrained belief that monogamy ensures a secure, harmonious, long-standing relationship. In truth, close to half of traditional marriages end in divorce—monogamy is no guarantee of commitment. Couples will also need to negotiate the limits of other relationships and how they divide their time between other partners. These logistic conversations can bring up intense feelings, especially early in the relationship. Couples therapy can support ENM partners in navigating these beliefs, emotions, and the conversations required to develop their relationship in a healthy way.

Communication Issues

People in ENM relationships can struggle with the same communication issues as those in monogamous relationships. If anything, the level of discourse about emotions, needs, and boundaries is higher in an ENM relationship than many monogamous relationships because there is an active negotiation of these things; rather than going along with traditional expectations from relationships, they are instead forging their own. But just because a couple has agreed to have a different relationship structure doesn't mean they won't also feel jealousy, insecurity, inadequacy, and other painful emotions. Even when all partners fully embrace this relationship structure, vulnerabilities and fears can be triggered in the process of creating it, and couples can fall into negative cycles as a result. In the healthiest ENM relationships, partners have space to disclose and process these feelings as they navigate how to pursue a satisfying relationship.

Infidelity

A common misconception is that infidelity is prevented by ethical non-monogamy. After all, how could someone cheat when everyone has agreed that it's acceptable to have other partners? The reality is that ENM relationships have many different structures and boundaries, and cheating *is* possible when one partner breaks the agreement or guidelines they have all consented to.

For example, perhaps two people in a primary partnership agree they can have sexual relationships with other people, but the sexual interaction can only happen one time with a given outside person. This would be to ensure that they aren't developing strong romantic partnerships outside their relationship without full awareness and agreement. If one partner sleeps with another person multiple times or starts dating them and keeping in contact between meetings, this would constitute infidelity.

Any healthy relationship, whether it be monogamous or ENM, is predicated on open communication and honesty; cheating happens when people have secrets and betray the relationship "contract." It's important that you understand this is just as hurtful and damaging in an ENM relationship as it is with monogamous couples. Addressing infidelity with a couple in an ENM relationship is similar to addressing it with a monogamous couple, which you'll learn about next.

Concluding Recommendations

In sum, the main recommendations for developing competency with ENM couples are to educate yourself, challenge your assumptions, seek supervision, and learn to affirm these relationships (Kisler & Lock, 2019). In chapter 11, you'll find recommendations for books on this topic. If you decide to make this a specialty in your practice, you should consider pursuing additional ENM-specific trainings.

Infidelity

Infidelity is a relatively common issue that couples face, yet many clinicians feel unprepared to help their clients work through this presenting problem because they lack adequate education and training to treat it (Irvine & Peluso, 2022). This is problematic given how prevalent infidelity is. Estimates suggest that between 20 and 40 percent of couples will experience at least one partner engaging in an affair or cheating at some point in their relationship. In the United States, the lifetime rate of infidelity is 20 to 25 percent for men and 11 to 15 percent for women (Wang, 2018).

While many people see cheating as an initial or principal relationship problem, research has shown that infidelity is usually a *symptom* of a relationship's issues rather than a primary cause (Gottman & Silver, 2012). In other words, people tend to seek intimacy outside of their relationship when their relationship is already weakened (i.e., partnership has conflict, couple experiences avoidance or emotional disconnection, and important needs are not being met). People who cheat usually first try to fix the problems with their partner and reestablish closeness and intimacy. Only when this doesn't work and they are lonely, frustrated, and hopeless do they go outside of the relationship to find comfort.

This isn't to excuse or justify infidelity, but rather to explain how it's not usually the first problem a relationship faces. It's important to know this because when couples start therapy following an infidelity, you'll be focusing on the affair first, while bearing in mind that there are earlier issues that must also be addressed if the couple is to heal and strengthen their relationship.

Like nonconventional relationships, infidelity is a triggering topic for many therapists. As a society, we have strong views about cheating. It is largely viewed as unforgivable, despite the fact that the majority of people will be impacted in some way by infidelity. Many therapists have themselves been unfaithful or been cheated on; even those without direct experience will have seen friends or family suffer the pain of infidelity. You may need to challenge some of your assumptions about infidelity and people who cheat before you begin working with couples in this situation. Hopefully, by seeing cheating as a symptom instead of a primary cause, and understanding the deep despair and pain that unfaithful partners typically endure prior to cheating, you will be able to empathize and compassionately work with unfaithful partners. However, if you determine that your countertransference is too high, it's perfectly acceptable to decide not to work with couples healing from infidelity; don't push yourself to work with any clients if you will not be able to see and hold them with empathy. We all have limits to our competence and comfort, and this may be one of yours. Knowing which clients and presenting problems you don't want to treat is important for all therapists. Use the following therapist reflection to explore your own feelings and assumptions about infidelity.

Therapist Reflection

Feelings and Assumptions about Infidelity

Infidelity, a common presenting problem in couples work, can bring up a range of responses from therapists. Take a moment to reflect on these questions, looking for possible biases or assumptions that you may need to challenge if you choose to work with couples healing from infidelity.

What are your automatic thoughts and feelings toward a person who has been unfaithful?

____

____

____

Do you think cheating is unforgivable? If your initial thought is no, are there any circumstances that would make you feel an instance of infidelity was unforgivable?

____

____

____

What are your instinctive thoughts and feelings toward the hurt partner who has decided to work on the relationship? What about a hurt partner who has decided to leave?

____

____

____

Would you judge someone for staying with their partner who has been unfaithful? What if their partner has cheated on them with multiple people, with someone they know, or for many years?

____

____

____

How might any personal experiences with infidelity influence your work with couples?

The Path to Healing

After the discovery of an affair, a couple can feel as though they are in freefall. Neither knows how to best navigate the rupture, their trust and connection is eroded, and they don't know where to turn for support. To best support these clients, offer them a roadmap of what healing will look like. According to Gottman's Trust Revival Method, there are three stages of healing after infidelity: atonement, attunement, and attachment (Gottman & Silver, 2012). These stages are similar to another model of healing an affair: reacting to the affair, reviewing options (to stay or leave), and recovering from the affair (Spring & Spring, 1996). As you'll notice in both approaches, the couple goes through an inevitable process of disclosure, followed by decision-making, and finally, healing or separating.

First, a couple must go through *disclosure* about the infidelity. Each will experience a cascade of painful emotions in this part of the process. The unfaithful partner needs to begin atoning in this stage if the couple is to move forward. In the second stage, couples begin exploring the contributions that led to the unfaithful partner's actions and the decision to stay and work on their relationship. Finally, in the third stage, the couple works to reestablish a secure attachment, which requires rebuilding trust and forgiveness. Looking more closely at each stage will help you understand goals for each part of the process as you support your clients through it.

Atonement Stage

In the *atonement stage* (also known as the crisis stage), one partner discovers the extent of the infidelity while the other expresses genuine remorse. *Genuine* is a key word here, because the partner who has been unfaithful must express authentic regret for their actions; otherwise, their partner will not feel reassured that the unfaithful partner won't cheat again. During this stage, there are intense feelings of hurt, betrayal, guilt, shame, and lack of trust. Triggers are abundant, as reminders of the infidelity seem to permeate every moment, and the resulting conversations are painful. In this stage, the unfaithful partner may feel "beat up" for their mistake, lose hope that their partner will ever forgive them, and fear their partner may decide to move on. Helping this client focus on taking responsibility, apologizing, and offering emotional support will help the couple move through this stage. You should also encourage the hurt partner to be open to the idea of forgiving the unfaithful person, even if they can't do it right now.

Attunement Stage

In the *attunement stage*, the couple examines their relationship prior to the affair to find what needs to be changed as they work toward building a stronger relationship. The couple aims to reestablish a secure attachment (or establishes it for the first time if they didn't feel secure in their relationship before) and works to identify and change their negative cycle of communication as they explore what led to the affair. Chances are (and research agrees) the infidelity didn't come out of nowhere—there were issues that led to one partner seeking comfort and intimacy from someone else, and this needs to be addressed. Often, couples have been disconnected or stuck in their negative cycle of communication for quite some time before one of them cheats. However, there are also cases where one person realizes that their own issues led to the affair, such as low self-esteem driving them to seek validation from others or substance abuse impacting their decision-making.

It's important to note that this stage isn't about assigning blame, especially not to the hurt partner. Some unfaithful partners who feel berated and beaten down during the atonement phase may see this next stage as an opportunity to shift blame to their partner and regain some standing in the relationship. However, blaming infidelity on the hurt partner by saying something like "If you had just [listened to me more; agreed to have more sex; spent more time with me], I wouldn't have cheated" is not a productive way to approach attunement. The hurt partner may indeed have missed important cues and failed to meet important needs, but while disconnection and misalignment explain an affair, they don't justify it. All partners contribute to the dysfunction in some way, so instead of blame seeking, help your clients look at this as a shared problem that they are solving together.

The attunement phase is when couples decide if they even can or want to move forward together. After learning about the details of the affair during atonement, they may decide it will be too difficult to heal and they would be better served amicably separating. This can be a good outcome for couples, especially when it is a mutual and kind decision. There is no prize for couples who stay together after an infidelity, and there is no failing grade for those who don't. It's simply a choice.

Attachment Stage

Finally, in the *attachment stage*, the couple has meaningful discussions about sex as they work to revive this part of their relationship. Many couples struggle to resume physical intimacy because of the vulnerability it requires, not to mention painful memories or intrusive thoughts that may arise. Talking about their fears and barriers to being sexual will help them to feel emotionally connected as they work toward how to feel safe being physically connected again. In this stage, couples also explore previously unearthed sexual needs and preferences, getting a better sense of each other's desires.

Other couples have sex quickly after discovering the affair, which can be confusing and surprising to even them. Wouldn't infidelity cause both partners to lose interest in being intimate? In fact, sex can be a way to reclaim connection and assert oneself as the primary partner to the other person. Intimacy can help the hurt partner feel wanted by their partner after the painful rejection of discovering infidelity and can give them a sense of togetherness. This desire for sex may not last long though, and couples still need to talk about their sexual needs so they can healthily and effectively reintroduce physical connection into their relationship.

It is important to assess how much of the infidelity, if any, was based in a discrepancy in sexual needs. Some couples are quick to blame these discrepancies when underlying disconnection and loneliness are the root of the infidelity. Other couples may have a strong emotional foundation in their relationship and simply lack the skills that they need to discuss sexual discrepancies. Either way, it is important that you remain aware that both sexual and emotional issues are likely at play—these will vary in degrees depending on the individual couple. To the extent that sexual needs discrepancies are present, the attachment phase will also include a great deal of discussion around sex and sexuality. For more on how to facilitate these discussions, see chapters 7 through 9.

Timeline for Healing

While each healing process is unique and timelines are hard to estimate, there are general phases and milestones in the healing process that indicate how far a couple has come in repairing from a rupture due to infidelity. Sharing these milestones can sometimes be helpful for couples who are feeling overwhelmed and hopeless, but it's vital to be clear with the couple that healing is not linear and that couples often move back and forth between stages. They may have a great day followed by three bad ones. They may have a month where they think they're past it, and then suddenly the intense feelings of betrayal and despair will return for a short time. Like grief, healing from infidelity can be unpredictable. The couple shouldn't panic when it feels like they've gone two steps back; it's just a part of the process.

Couples should also be aware that these milestones do not rigidly adhere to a schedule. Remind your clients that it's okay if they don't feel more stable in the relationship after three months. People heal differently, and timelines aren't intended to be an infallible marker of whether or not a relationship can survive an affair. Rather, timelines provide general guideposts for what healing looks like over the long term, helping couples see a path forward and regain some hope while keeping their expectations reasonable.

First Few Weeks After

During the discovery and crisis phase, when the infidelity is first disclosed, there should be a focus on gathering information and understanding what happened. This is a critical period of time for the couple; how they navigate the disclosure will impact the rest of their healing process. Understandably, the person who cheated may avoid answering painful questions, tell half-truths, or omit information in effort to protect their partner from further hurt. They may also feel immense guilt and shame about their behavior and have difficulty facing it.

To further complicate this process, there can be too much disclosure about information that is not necessary or helpful for the healing process. These "detective questions," as termed by therapist Esther Perel (2017), provide sordid details of the affair that do not help the hurt partner understand the underlying reasons for why it happened. These questions paint a painfully vivid picture of what the unfaithful partner did, which the hurt partner cannot unsee. Although many hurt partners want to know these types of specific details, they can be counterproductive to healing. According to Perel (2017), the better approach to understanding why the affair happened involves "investigative questions." These questions explore the motivation and meaning behind the infidelity and seek to gain an understanding of why it happened and how the unfaithful partner felt during the experience. This approach looks at the infidelity in the context of the relationship and helps the hurt partner figure out if they want to stay in the relationship. If they do, it will provide a roadmap for what needs to be healed and changed for the couple to move forward.

Three to Six Months After

This is a time of intense emotions, lack of trust, hurt, and rupture, particularly during the early weeks and months. The infidelity will be top of your clients' minds and it will be hard for them to think or talk about much else. They will feel consumed with intense emotions and what feels like constant conversations about it. This will be a time for you to support them in ensuring they have emotion regulation skills and social support, as well as remind them that this phase does not last forever.

During this time, it's helpful for the unfaithful partner to be the one to carry the emotional burden of bringing up the affair by asking their partner how they are feeling. In doing so, they show their commitment to taking care of the hurt partner and provide reassurance that they don't think the hurt partner should be over their pain.

After six months, the wound is still deep, but clients may begin to feel more stable in their relationship and more functional in their daily lives. The infidelity will still come up frequently, but it may be easier to talk about. This is because there is no more uncovering and early processing to be done; instead, your clients are able to engage more deeply about why the infidelity happened and how they plan to heal from it together. For this reason, many recommend that couples try to wait six months before deciding whether they want to stay together or not; by this time, they'll have a better sense if their relationship can recover from the infidelity and if they want to be together.

One Year After

After a year of working through the rupture in trust, your clients may be feeling more positive about their relationship. The couple should have engaged in deep conversations about why the affair happened, what it meant to each of them, and how to move forward together. However, the one-year-mark is challenging because the infidelity will resurface as the anniversary triggers painful memories of its discovery. It's critical that you anticipate this and ensure your clients are sufficiently prepared for possible emotions they'll experience and intentional about how they will manage this time in their relationship.

Two Years After and Beyond

The consensus among professionals is that the average couple may feel they have healed from an affair by the two-year mark. By this time, if your clients have been successful in working through the affair, they will likely feel recommitted, stable, and secure. This doesn't mean triggers won't bring back painful emotions or memories, but they will be able to navigate those times with open communication and connection. For very successful couples, they will feel stronger for having worked through the painful rupture they experienced, and even more confident that they can tackle challenges together.

Common Challenges

Healing from infidelity is a difficult process, and there are several common feelings and barriers that make it even more so. You'll see your clients struggle with these barriers, so knowing that they will arise and what to do about them is critical. Perhaps the best support you can give your clients is the reassurance that these challenges are normal and can be worked through, but also that they don't have to be worked through. Some people can get through the painful feelings and others can't.

Fear of Judgment for Staying

Some hurt partners are afraid that family or friends will judge them for staying in a relationship where their partner cheated. This is why hurt partners need to be very intentional about whom they disclose the infidelity to. A friend may be more understanding and helpful than, say, a parent who will never look at their partner the same way. Infidelity doesn't need to be a shameful secret that is kept strictly within the relationship, but your clients need to consider if the people they seek support from will be empathic and helpful, or if they will have strong opinions that could sway your clients one way or another. Healing from infidelity is hard enough without having to convince friends and family that it was a valid choice for the hurt partner and that they can forgive the unfaithful partner.

Struggles in the Atonement Stage

The unfaithful partner will understandably struggle during the atonement stage of healing. They will have to answer painful questions (often repeatedly), endure their partner's intense emotions, endure their own intense emotions, and make amends over and over. This is no easy task. Unfaithful partners often feel guilt and shame, and having their partner bring up the affair with anger and hurt only amplifies those emotions. Further, the unfaithful partner was likely unhappy in the relationship prior to cheating but must put their unmet needs aside while they focus on the more urgent issue of affair recovery. This is why infidelity makes change so hard: it puts other critical issues on the back burner, and not every unfaithful partner has the patience or willingness to do that. One way to ensure the unfaithful partner stays committed to the process is to be empathic toward them from the start, helping them identify the problems that led to their choice and reassuring them that these problems will be a focus in therapy once the acute phase of healing is over.

Likewise, the hurt partner will struggle with this stage of healing. They will experience an intense rollercoaster of emotions that will dominate their mood. Some may feel incapacitated by it, struggling to work, sleep, or eat. They may have intrusive thoughts and sudden bouts of rage or sadness, made worse by the fact that the person they usually turn to for emotional support is the one who caused them this suffering.

In the throes of early healing, it can be hard to see an end to the pain. You can reassure your clients that the intensity and volatility of their emotions will not last forever. Eventually, they will be able to think and talk about the affair with less acute distress. You should encourage the unfaithful partner to be patient and understanding, as any attempts to rush the hurt partner to "get over it" will only lengthen this process because they will feel their partner is minimizing or judging their experience.

Lack of Trust

Infidelity erodes a couple's foundation of trust, and regaining trust is a challenging and lengthy process. Once it has been broken, the hurt partner will wonder why they should (and how they *could*) trust again, especially with the lingering fear that their partner may cheat again. Words of commitment and reassurances from the unfaithful partner are important, but the only real assurance comes from the partner choosing not to cheat again, and that takes time to see and believe. Remind your clients that one element of the healing journey is simply the passage of time. If the hurt partner still feels distrustful after six months or a year, perhaps it's time to reevaluate the decision to stay together.

Sacrifices

Many couples feel uncomfortable with the sacrifices necessary to reestablish trust and prioritize their relationship. However, for such a significant rupture to be healed, the unfaithful partner will have to give up things they otherwise wouldn't need to. The common example is that the unfaithful partner may need to forgo some privacy as trust is rebuilt, such as allowing their partner to access their phone or sharing their location. Other sacrifices include ending all contact with the affair partner and anyone in that person's social circle, limiting travel, and changing activities or jobs if they are associated with the affair partner. The unfaithful partner may dislike giving these things up, even temporarily, and the hurt partner may dislike asking for these changes just as much. These are accommodations you wouldn't usually want couples to make, but they must do so when they are healing from infidelity. Remind your clients that these changes show a commitment to the relationship, and many are temporary ways of rebuilding trust. Also, encourage them to consider the choice they have in asking for or implementing these changes. No one is forced to comply, but rather they may willingly shift parts of their relationship as they reestablish their foundation.

Remember to Instill Hope

Couples healing from infidelity are in a fragile place. They are usually hurt, scared, and hopeless. They have been brave enough to seek help as they work on their relationship, and your role is to give them clear advice and imbue hope. As the expert, you know more than they do about what healing involves and what they should do to repair the rupture as effectively as possible. Be in charge, be comforting, provide actionable advice, and offer hope. Perhaps the best way of framing hope for your clients is by explaining that their original relationship is now over, and they are beginning a new one together. Their old relationship had good parts but also major problems, and through this healing process they are creating a new, stronger relationship together. They will learn new skills, such as how to communicate more effectively, that will benefit them for the rest of their lives.

Discernment Counseling

Most often, couples seeking therapy are committed to working on their relationship because they want to be together. However, some couples are a better fit for *discernment counseling*, where the therapist creates a supportive holding environment while helping couples determine if they want to stay together or separate. In these so-termed "mixed-agenda couples," one person wants to continue the relationship while the other is ambivalent or wants to end the relationship.

Although couples therapy theories and interventions often focus on the couples who have a mutual desire for positive change, mixed-agenda couples account for somewhere near 30 percent of those who seek clinical help, so it's important to understand what these couples need and how to support them (Doherty, 2011; Doherty et al., 2016). This section will give you a brief overview of key points within discernment counseling, but if you decide to pursue this nuanced area of couples work, you will certainly benefit from further education and training.

Setting a Timeline

A significant contributing factor to your clients' pain is not knowing how long they will remain in this relationship limbo. This uncertainty is hard for all partners, even those who are ambivalent about the relationship. One way to address this is to help your clients decide on a brief timeline. It doesn't need to be definitive, but having a general sense of how long they will engage in discernment counseling before making a decision about the relationship can ease some of the anxiety that "this will last forever." For discernment counseling, this timeline is short—one to five sessions is recommended. For example, the couple might agree to four initial sessions: one joint session, two individual sessions, and one joint session after. This brief timeline highlights how discernment counseling is not intended to be a lengthy process; rather, it is short-term work to help a couple decide which path to take.

Key Aspects of Early Sessions

With mixed-agenda couples, you only have a few sessions (perhaps only one) to ascertain what your clients want. As always, your first task is to establish rapport with all clients, regardless of how invested they are in the relationship or the discernment process. Showing understanding and empathy to all clients will help them feel seen and safe during a time that stirs up feelings of insecurity and pain. And remember, even the ambivalent partner is struggling; although it seems like they have the "power" in the relationship, many uncertain partners feel incredibly torn and confused about what to do, fearful of making the wrong decision or an irreversible mistake and thus ruining one or both of their lives.

However, establishing rapport can be challenging, as you're dealing with clients who have very different views about the relationship. Therapists can fall into one of three traps during the early stages: immediately trying to convince a couple to commit to therapy for a period of time (thus allying with the committed partner), insisting the couple make their decision before helping them do any meaningful work, or only meeting in conjoined sessions instead of having individual meetings (Doherty & Harris, 2017). You need to ensure that all partners feel seen and understood, not pressured or judged, and able to speak honestly about their feelings and fears.

As you establish rapport, you should focus on deeply understanding how each partner feels about the relationship. You can't help them navigate their mixed agenda if you don't know exactly what each person's agenda is. How invested are they in continuing the relationship? What are the problems and barriers to being together? What needs to change for them to feel confident staying with their partner? This is when individual sessions are critical, as it allows each client to speak openly about their feelings, fears, and needs when it comes to continuing the relationship.

Remember that your job is to help them gain clarity about the decision they are facing. You are not engaging in couples therapy because the couple hasn't decided whether that's the path they will take. Jumping into healing their relationship could end up doing more harm than good, such as alienating the ambivalent partner. Your role is to support them in deciding whether they think they can and want to do couples work.

Finally, it's of paramount importance that clients feel their participation in counseling is a choice—and one they can continue to make. This means engaging your clients at the end of each session in deciding whether they want to schedule another one (or several) and ensuring they do not feel pressured to say yes. Part of this process is supporting your clients in determining whether they want to put time and effort into the relationship in small doses.

The Three Paths Forward

When mixed-agenda couples come to you, they are feeling lost and upset. The first thing you can offer them is information about the process of counseling and the three possible outcomes. The first outcome is that they stay together in the status quo of their relationship; they don't make any changes to their dynamics and continue on as they have been. The second path is to end the relationship, and the third is to continue couples counseling with the goal of changing their relationship for the better. The goal of discernment counseling is to help your clients decide with confidence and clarity which path they'd like to pursue (Doherty & Harris, 2017).

Path One: The Status Quo

Some couples will see you briefly and decide to continue the relationship without committing to couples therapy. These couples are fearful of the relationship ending but unwilling (or unable) to put work into making changes that would benefit them. Sometimes these couples have a "wake-up call" just by attending one or two sessions, realizing that they actually don't want to leave their partner and gaining a renewed sense of appreciation for the relationship they almost lost. Other times, these couples are not ready for the work required to improve the relationship and feel comfortable staying with the status quo even if they aren't very happy in it. If couples choose this path, there isn't much you can do besides offering to work together in the future should they change their minds and wishing them the best. Having a positive therapy experience makes it more likely they will seek help again, and knowing your door is open will make it easier for them to reach out.

There are also situations where just mentioning this path as an option makes your clients realize they are aligned in not wanting things to stay as they are. The ambivalent partner clearly wants change, but they may not realize the committed partner also wants the relationship to improve and won't be happy with things continuing on as they have been. This can renew their investment in making change together (Doherty & Harris, 2017).

Path Two: Ending the Relationship

This is a painful path to bear witness to, especially if not all partners agree to this decision. While staying together requires all partners to agree, breaking up only needs one person to make that choice. Indeed, endings are not often mutually agreed upon. But remember, for some couples, an ending is the best choice, at least for one of the partners. Not every relationship can be saved, and sometimes it's best for your clients to amicably part instead of fighting for a union that isn't serving one or all of them. Discernment counseling can still greatly benefit the couples who choose this path, as some research shows couples found counseling helpful in navigating the decision-making process and empowered them for better communication and coparenting after the divorce (Emerson et al., 2021).

As the therapist, you can serve an important role when couples decide to end their relationship. You can support them as they process their feelings (there will be many conflicting and intense emotions) and navigate the logistics of separation. Often couples will stop counseling once they decide to separate, but you may have time in a final session to reinforce their work and give a brief roadmap of what to expect, which includes a rollercoaster of emotions as they process the breakup, tell people in their lives, and disentangle any administrative and legal work involved with a split.

Path Three: Committing to Change

When clients decide to stay together and work on their relationship, your work will shift from discernment counseling to couples therapy. No longer will you be weighing pros and cons of staying versus leaving; now you will be helping your clients identify their negative cycle, break bad habits of interacting, and build a new, stronger relationship. It's worth noting that you can also refer the couple to another therapist for this work should you decide you are not the right fit after offering discernment counseling.

It's best if your clients can agree to take a breakup or divorce off the table for a specified amount of time. This is because it's difficult for couples to engage openly and authentically as they work on the relationship if they think their partner still has one foot out the door. If they're working with you, it means they have some level of interest in or commitment to each other; to give their relationship fair consideration, they need to not live in fear that their partner could leave them at any second. Six months is a good length of time for clients to commit to working on the relationship before revisiting the question of a breakup (Doherty & Harris, 2017).

All that being said, your clients do not have to stay together for the duration of the timeline they agreed to. If they realize midway through the process of couples therapy that they want to leave, they most certainly can. In fact, it would be hurtful for them to stay if they knew that the relationship was over for them. If any partner wants to end the relationship before the previously determined timeline of couples work, they should share this decision with kindness and gentleness. If you ever suspect a client is wavering in their decision to work on the relationship, you can always schedule individual sessions to again gauge the motivation and commitment of each partner.

Key Takeaways

Discernment counseling is different in that it's short term (one to five sessions) with a clear goal of helping clients decide which of three paths to take: staying together in the status quo, breakup or divorce, or working on the relationship for at least six months. Your focus should be on building rapport and ensuring clients are freely engaging in the discernment process. If your clients decide to stay together and work on the relationship, you then shift your work into couples therapy, where the goals are markedly different from discernment counseling. Always keep in mind that there is no "right" choice for mixed-agenda couples. Although most couples therapists hope their clients will stay together, sometimes it's best (or unavoidable) that a relationship ends.

Abuse in Relationships

As you know from chapter 2, abusive relationships are contraindicated for couples therapy because these couples shouldn't be kept together; working with these couples can actually make things worse. However, it's important to know what an abusive relationship looks like and where the line is between couples who are behaving badly and couples who are stuck in the cycle of abuse.

Emotional, Physical, and Sexual Abuse

Although there are many types of abuse, we will be looking at three main kinds that you may observe in your work: emotional, physical, and sexual. Knowing what abuse looks like in these three areas can help you better identify when abuse is occurring.

In all relationships, people have boundaries. There are many kinds of boundaries, such as emotional, physical, and financial, among others. In healthy relationships, people respect each other's boundaries. They don't knowingly cross the other's boundaries without consent or a very, very good reason. Sometimes partners do cross boundaries with justification, such as someone taking financial control from a partner in a manic episode who is spending all their money. But these situations are not frequent, and as a general rule, partners should respect each other's limits.

As obvious as it may seem, an important part of boundaries is clearly communicating them. A partner can't know if they have crossed a line if they didn't know the line existed in the first place. This doesn't mean your clients need to sit down and list out all the boundaries they have, but it does mean your clients need to say when their partner has crossed a boundary with them. This way, their partner can be aware of this limit and respect it in the future. People who knowingly and repeatedly cross their partner's boundaries, whether through lack of care or through justification (e.g., "they deserved it"), are edging toward or fully engaging in abusive behaviors.

Physical Abuse

Physical abuse is the violation of someone's physical boundaries, or making someone feel physically threatened, hurt, or unsafe. Violating these boundaries can look like touching someone when they don't want to be touched, physically restraining someone, blocking someone's path when they're trying to move, or being aggressive or violent in any way.

There are certain undeniable physical boundaries that should never be crossed; other physical boundaries can vary from person to person. Regarding the former, there is a baseline expectation that people should feel physically safe in their relationship. Your clients should have assurance that no matter how heated an argument may get, they will always be physically safe with their partner. Behaviors that are unacceptable include throwing items at the other person; punching near them; blocking their exit; trapping them somewhere; or physically harming them in ways such as hitting, kicking, or restraining. People should feel they have control and autonomy over their body and environment. In other words, they should not be physically hurt or restrained. Not wanting a hug from a partner is one thing; feeling scared that a partner will be violent is another.

There are also personal preferences for physical boundaries. For example, some people dislike any physical touch when they're upset, while others seek closeness. It's important for your clients to know and share their physical needs and limits. Remember, couples need to communicate what their boundaries are *in the moment*, such as telling their partner that they don't want a hug, because their partner may not know they don't want to be physically comforted. Remind your clients that partners are not mind readers—their partner cannot know what they want or don't want unless they say so directly. If one partner gives the other a hug when they wanted to be left alone, but the partner being hugged did not share that it was unwanted, this is not, in itself, a boundary violation. If your clients' partners don't know their needs and limits, they can't be expected to magically honor them.

Emotional Abuse

Emotional abuse is the recurring violation of the needs and limits people have that make them feel safe. These boundaries are what people are willing to both give and receive emotionally. These boundaries are sometimes harder for people to identify in themselves, and thus harder for their partners to know about too. Individual therapy can support people in understanding their emotional boundaries, so if you're working with a client who truly doesn't know these needs or limits, it may be good to recommend individual work.

Along with individualized emotional boundaries, there are also general emotional boundaries that are true for all people; no one should be cruelly embarrassed or have their reality questioned. Behaviors and actions such as gaslighting, mocking, denigrating, ignoring, stonewalling, shaming, publicly embarrassing, manipulating, yelling, screaming, blaming, isolating, constant monitoring, controlling, being excessively jealous, and humiliating the other person are all considered emotional abuse. People shouldn't need to explicitly state these emotional boundaries because everyone should be treated with this baseline of respect. However, it can be helpful for you to point out any emotional boundary violations you witness and explain why they're unacceptable. Emotional abuse can be incredibly damaging and have long-term effects for the victim, causing them to lose their sense of identity, self-trust, and self-worth.

In abusive relationships, emotional boundary violations happen frequently and insidiously. However, it can be difficult to spot them, especially if the abusive partner is adept at explaining away the violation. The abusive partner may say they were more hurt than the victim and insist that it justified the violation, or they might gaslight their partner into thinking the violation didn't even happen. On the other side of the equation, many victims of emotional abuse don't recognize that emotional boundary violations have happened, let alone what to do about it, which can make them quite vulnerable. When looking for emotional boundary crossings, trust your instinct. Even if the partner who was violated doesn't feel upset, it's not an indication that what happened is acceptable.

Sexual Abuse

Sexual abuse covers a wide range of behaviors. In short, sexual abuse is any sexual act that occurs without true consent. (For more on true consent, see chapter 9.) The most apparent forms of sexual abuse occur when a sexual act, such as intercourse, outercourse, or touching of private areas, happens with protest, under duress, or without actual consent. However, sexual abuse can take more covert forms. For example, if a person uses punishment or coercion to "turn a no into a yes," that is sexual abuse. Sexual abuse can even be verbal, such as making sexual comments or jokes in an environment where it is unwanted (e.g., at work, in public). Because sexual abuse can be so nuanced, like other forms of abuse, it may take time to assess whether or not it is present.

Cycle of Abuse

Abusive relationships are characterized by a cycle of abuse that can become worse over time. It is similar to the healthy cycle of harmony-rupture-repair, except it is extreme and destructive. The abuse cycle's stages are *tension, abuse incident, reconciliation*, and *calm* (Walker, 1979/2005). Sometimes the stages occur in different orders to different degrees, and the type of abuse may change from incident to incident, but relationships with cyclical abuse generally follow this pattern. Each stage of the cycle will be discussed in more depth so that you can be better equipped to identify them.

Building Tension

In this phase, there is a slow build of irritation and tension. The abusive partner becomes increasingly annoyed, impatient, and upset over small things. They blame their partner for this irritation, refusing to take any responsibility themselves. Their partner feels as though they are walking on eggshells in the relationship, and everything they do or say ends up being wrong and a source of anger.

Abuse Incident

After the tension builds, the abuse finally occurs when the abusive partner attempts to regain a sense of power. At the start of an abusive relationship, incidents are often less blatantly unacceptable, such as yelling, blaming, or hitting a wall without harming the other. But over time, abuse incidents can become more and more extreme and dangerous, including social isolation, breaking items in the home, humiliation, and physical violence.

Reconciliation

Following the outburst, the abusive partner attempts to reconcile and amend what they've done. They may take responsibility, appear genuinely remorseful, apologize, and promise never to do it again. The abusive partner often showers their partner with love and affection to keep them from leaving. This is when a tactic called *love bombing* often occurs, in which the abusive partner provides excessive affection, praise, and even gifts to "atone" for the abuse incident.

Calm

At the end of this cycle is calm. Things return to normal, with both partners feeling relatively positive about their relationship. This period of tentative peace does not last for long. Although there is no acute disconnection or anxiety in the relationship, the abusive partner's remorse and doting behavior fade away.

As tension begins building again, the abusive partner may shift from being apologetic about their violent behavior to justifying it or blaming their partner for it.

Working with Couples in Problematic Relationships

Couples seeking therapy are likely engaging in unhelpful behaviors and may even fall into abusive territory. This is true even for some couples with healthy, self-aware partners. It is crucial for you to learn the line between unhealthy but workable relationships, and abusive but unsavable relationships. Once you know which type of relationship you're working with, you can decide the best course of action.

Assessing Couples for Abuse

As you know from chapter 1, there are many important aspects to assessing new couples. When assessing for abuse, you need to look for safety, self-awareness, accountability, and desire to change. First and foremost is safety; if you think a person in the relationship is not physically or emotionally safe, they are not a couple you should be working with at this time. Physical violence is a hard line; when there is any physical violence, it's best to ensure the partner has support through individual therapy and can make a safety plan that their abusive partner doesn't know about. However, if couples are engaging in destructive behaviors (outside of physical violence) but have insight, hold themselves responsible, and want to change how they act, they may be a good fit for therapy.

Sometimes it's hard to identify abuse, particularly if the couple has been in a long relationship and emotional abuse has slowly built up over time. Trust your gut during the assessment. If a client is saying all the right things but you have a feeling that something isn't quite right, trust that feeling. If there's ever a question about safety, or if a relationship is abusive, you need to do individual sessions so you can find out more. Assessments won't always be completed in the first few sessions, but you should keep the assessment mindset with couples where the health and safety of the relationship isn't clear. Once you identify a pattern of abuse that can't or shouldn't be treated in couples therapy, it's time to act, no matter how long it took to notice the issue.

Identifying Abusive Partners

Abusive people lack self-awareness and self-control. They are overwhelmed by their painful feelings, and the only way they know to manage those feelings is through blame. You'll see this when clients consistently blame their partner for every painful feeling they experience, such as claiming they wouldn't get angry or withdraw if their partner would simply stop doing things wrong all the time. For example, when these clients feel jealous, they blame their partner for being unfaithful. When they feel lonely, they blame their partner for not spending enough time with them. And when they're upset that the house is messy, they blame their partner for not cleaning.

You'll be able to spot abusive partners by how they use the blame to justify their inexcusable actions. They feel that their behavior is justified because of how awful the other person "made" them feel. They're unable to take responsibility for their own feelings, let alone take responsibility for the actions stemming from those feelings. They live in a victim mindset where people hurt them and they need to lash out to defend themselves. Because of this fragility, they often struggle to gain the insight and empowerment needed to own their feelings, be accountable for their actions, and learn new ways of expressing their pain.

To make things more confusing, it's not uncommon for abusive partners to be the ones to claim the other is abusive. If you have a client who keeps blaming their partner for everything, refuses to take any responsibility, or outright labels their partner as abusive (or uses other clinically loaded terms in session such as saying their partner gaslights them, is a narcissist, etc.), you should pause. This can be a tactic used by abusive partners to make their partner appear less believable and even seem like the abuser. This tactic is known as *DARVO*: the abusive partner **d**enies the abuse, **a**ttacks their partner for accusing them of abuse, and then **r**everses the roles of **v**ictim and **o**ffender by pointing to their partner as the perpetrator of abuse in the relationship.

Providing Referrals

For couples in abusive relationships, your first action should be providing referrals. This can be done jointly or separately depending on how concerned you are for the partner who is being subjected to abuse. Recommending individual therapy for both partners is a good first step. For abusive relationships where safety is a concern, you should also recommend additional resources to the survivor, such as the National Domestic Violence Hotline, which can provide additional information and support. While you don't want to work with couples in abusive situations for reasons previously noted, you also don't want to leave them (especially the victim) with no support.

Working with Borderline Cases

If you're working with a couple where some abusive behaviors are occurring but your clients express true remorse and a desire to change, they may be able to continue the work. Some clients do not realize their actions count as abuse and are ashamed to realize it; even though learning the skills to better manage their feelings may be challenging, they can and want to change. There are a few things to know and do when working with these types of couples.

First, you must label the behaviors as abusive. This can be done with compassion and is not intended to incur shame, but rather to show your clients where the line is in how they treat each other. Acknowledge that many people (perhaps most) engage in behaviors that are considered abusive at one time or another, but knowing what's unacceptable helps them make different choices, apologize, and repair if or when they transgress.

Next, you need to establish ground rules and have your clients agree to them. During and outside of session, they cannot engage in abusive behaviors with each other. If they drift into that territory during heightened moments, then they need to agree that they will remove themselves from the situation until they're calm. They also need to enlist more support in managing their feelings through therapy or an anger management group. Finally, you can require open communication with their individual therapists as a precondition for continuing treatment.

Remember that you are continuing your assessment of your clients' relationship even if you agree to keep working with them. Some lapses may occur, but if they recognize the regression and both appear to make a genuine effort to get back on track, they may still be a good fit. However, if you notice a persistent increase in abusive behaviors, they are not a good fit for couples therapy. If this happens, you need to be clear about your concerns that their relationship isn't healthy or safe and explain that continuing individual therapy is your recommended course of action.

Finally, you may see a client try to leave an abusive partner during your work. When an abusive person's partner makes a real attempt to leave, it can go two ways. One way is that the abusive partner may express sudden insight into their behavior and proclaim a desire to change. This is also a common place for couples to start therapy. The other path is that the abusive partner becomes enraged and even more threatening, making it scary or unsafe for their partner to leave them. This is why working with couples who are in truly abusive relationships is contraindicated; having abusive partners be part of the breakup process can be life-threatening.

Seeking Supervision

Assessing and working with possibly abusive relationships is incredibly difficult. Even seasoned therapists can miss the signs and begin or continue to work with a couple caught in the cycle of abuse; others have labeled couples as unsavable when that wasn't the case. Although being able to assess this is a critical skill to develop, you're not supposed to be an infallible abuse detector. Especially for early-stage clinicians or those who are new to this type of work, supervision will be invaluable. Seek an individual supervisor or join a group supervision so you have other therapists to support you in this learning process.

Other Topics to Consider Exploring

In addition to the special topics mentioned in this chapter, many clinicians decide to specialize further in couples work by pursuing other possible presenting problems or niches commonly seen in clinical work. The following list includes a number of these specific topics, though it is certainly not an exhaustive list:

- Working through parenting challenges or navigating life after kids are raised ("empty nest syndrome")
- Deciding whether or not to get married
- Navigating other major life decisions (e.g., career shifts, moving)
- Dealing with acute mental health or medical conditions (e.g., addiction, neurodiversity)

- Struggling with infertility
- Managing challenges of a long-distance relationship
- Navigating individual trauma in their relationship
- Joining or leaving a faith or religious community
- Navigating postpartum life with newborns or young children
- Dealing with complicated immediate or extended family situations

In the next chapter, you will learn about sex therapy, which includes more special topics and subspecialties as well. Chapter 7 will begin exploring why sex is such an important topic in couples work, including its benefits and the reasons couples seek it out. This chapter may lead you to uncover some latent biases or discomforts with the topic, as is common in many therapists.

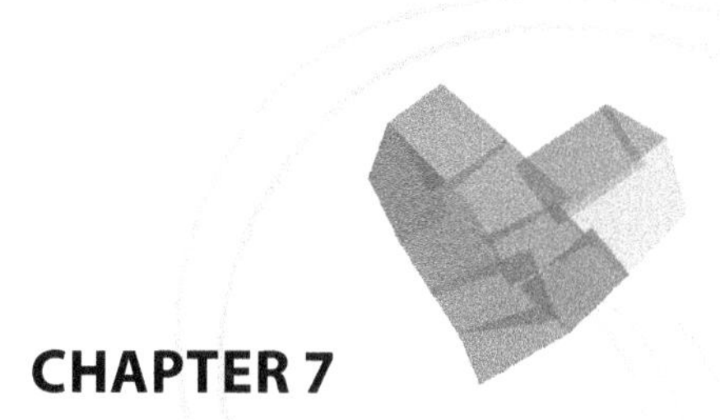

CHAPTER 7

The Importance of Sex

Sex can be many things—intimate, loving, fun, silly, confusing, or even traumatic. It can leave us feeling elated, loved, powerful, sad, used, or lonely. Sexuality is a biopsychosocial trait, meaning that it is influenced by biology, psychology, emotions, and factors like society, culture, and our relationships. In short, sex is complicated. So why do we do it? Why are so many people drawn to sexual expression and behavior? In this chapter, you will learn to help your clients examine both the benefits of and the motivations for engaging in sexual behavior.

The Benefits of Sex

Let's begin with the benefits of positive sexual experiences. First, let's make sure that we are talking about the same thing. Many people use the term *sex* interchangeably with *intercourse*. However, sex is an umbrella term that encompasses a wide variety of behavior. Any behavior that holds erotic value for a person could be considered sex, such as giving or receiving oral or manual stimulation of genital or erogenous zones. When considering the benefits of positive sexual experiences, keep in mind that "sex" extends far beyond simple intercourse.

Biological Benefits

Sexual health and satisfaction are important determinants of physical health and overall well-being. Research shows that sex boosts the functioning of our immune system (Rogers, 2018) and cognitive system (Allen, 2018). In other words, sex helps us heal and fight off illness more effectively as well as think analytically and improve memory. There is also evidence to suggest that sexual behavior improves sleep and even provides headache and migraine relief. Furthermore, sex is associated with lower blood pressure and a lower risk of heart attack, stroke (Liu et al., 2016), incontinence in women, and prostate cancer in men.

Emotional and Psychological Benefits

Have your clients ever wondered why they might feel more relaxed and secure after sex? Perhaps they sleep better or feel more positive about themselves and their life. Pleasurable sexual behavior can have a myriad of emotional and psychological benefits. Broadly, positive sexual experiences can improve our mental well-being (Debro et al., 2017). They boost self-esteem and expand our ability to perceive, identify, and express emotions. Sex can also decrease stress, soothe anxiety, and promote relaxation through its effects on various biochemicals, such as lowering cortisol and releasing oxytocin, dopamine, vasopressin, and prolactin. In addition, sex helps meet our psychological needs for safety and connection.

Relational Benefits

Relational benefits refer to outcomes that positively affect our relationships. Hopefully, your clients have had the experience of feeling more connected to their partner after being sexual with them. This is because partnered sexual activity can strengthen levels of trust, intimacy, and love. This isn't just a feeling—it's science! As mentioned previously, the chemicals released by sexual activity, specifically oxytocin and vasopressin, promote connection and bonding between partners.

Motivations for Sexual Behavior

While there are many benefits to sexual behavior, these benefits aren't always what we're seeking when we engage in sex. What is it, then, that motivates us to have sex?

Meston, Stanton, and Buss (2020) studied motivations for sex and broke them down into four main categories: *physical, emotional, goal attainment*, and *insecurity soothing*. Sex provides physical sensations, such as touch and pleasure, as well as emotional sensations, such as intimacy and closeness. Sex can also be used to attain goals, such as pregnancy, or soothe insecurities by providing validation that we are attractive or loved.

Because sex is so complex, so are our reasons for engaging in it. Moreover, we have a tendency to make value judgments around motivations for sex, holding some motivations as "better" and others as "worse." Take a moment to think about your own sexual experiences. What are the reasons that you've engaged in sexual activity in the past? Notice your reactions to your own motivations—what reasons led you to judge yourself? Which reasons do you deem acceptable, and which reasons do you deem shameful?

Now imagine that your clients are coming to you with similar experiences. Use the following activity to help them understand more about their motivations for being sexual.

Client Activity

Motivations for Sex*

Separately, take a few minutes to think about your past and present sexual relationships. What role has sex played in your relationships? Specifically, what motivated you to have sex in these relationships?

Review the following categories of motivations for sex and place a check mark on each item that describes your sexual experiences. Be kind to yourself and push aside any self-judgment that may arise. Our cultural environment often teaches us that there are "good" and "bad" reasons to have sex. For this activity, let that judgment go and respond honestly. Remember, you're here to improve your understanding of yourself, and for that, you need accurate, honest data.

Physical Reasons

- ☐ Wanted to reduce anxiety or stress
- ☐ Wanted to release tension or frustration
- ☐ Hadn't had sex in a while and it was on my mind
- ☐ Wanted to feel healthy
- ☐ Felt horny and wanted an orgasm
- ☐ Wanted to do something exciting or adventurous
- ☐ Wanted to experience pleasure
- ☐ Person was physically attractive
- ☐ Person was irresistible
- ☐ Person did something attractive
- ☐ Wanted to see what it was like
- ☐ Wanted to improve sexual techniques

Goal Attainment

- ☐ Wanted to get compensated in some way
- ☐ Wanted to punish myself

* This activity is adapted with permission from "The Why Have Sex? Questionnaire," in R. R. Milhausen, J. K. Sakaluk, T. D. Fisher, C. M. Davis, and W. L. Yarber (Eds.), *Handbook of Sexuality-Related Measures*, 4th ed. (p. 473), by C. M. Meston, A. M. Stanton, and D. M. Buss, 2020, Routledge.

- ☐ Wanted to reproduce
- ☐ Wanted to enhance my reputation
- ☐ Would have damaged my reputation to say no
- ☐ Responded to a dare
- ☐ Wanted to get back at my partner for cheating
- ☐ Was on the "rebound"
- ☐ Wanted to hurt another person or relationship
- ☐ Wanted to get out of a conversation or activity
- ☐ Helped me fall asleep
- ☐ Wanted to get or pay back a favor

Emotional Reasons

- ☐ Wanted to express my affection or love
- ☐ Wanted to deepen my connection
- ☐ Knew I was in love
- ☐ Wanted to celebrate
- ☐ Wanted my partner to feel good
- ☐ Wanted to say something (e.g., I'm sorry, thank you)
- ☐ Wanted to increase emotional bond
- ☐ Desired emotional closeness
- ☐ Wanted my partner to feel good about themselves
- ☐ Seemed like the next step in the relationship
- ☐ Wanted to welcome my partner home or say goodbye
- ☐ Wanted my partner to express love

Insecurity Soothing

- ☐ Wanted to feel good about myself
- ☐ Wanted to feel powerful
- ☐ Wanted attention
- ☐ Didn't want to disappoint the person or feel guilty
- ☐ Didn't know how to say no
- ☐ Felt pressured, obligated, or forced to

- ☐ Wanted to keep my partner from cheating or leaving me
- ☐ Wanted to feel secure in relationship
- ☐ Wanted the person to love me
- ☐ Wanted to be nice
- ☐ Wanted to ensure the relationship was committed
- ☐ Thought it would help solidify a new relationship

After you've completed the questionnaire, examine your responses. Do you notice any patterns? Did some items describe a lot of your experiences, some, or just a few? Did you check off more in one category than the others?

Motivations for Sex Debrief

Discuss the results of the *Motivations for Sex* activity with your clients. Which category did they check the most boxes? Is there much variability between their scores in each category, or are the scores relatively even? Are they surprised by their results or those of their partner? Notice how each client feels about their results and the results of their partner. Do you notice anyone separating motivations for sex into "good" and "bad" categories?

This activity is an opportunity to explore your clients' motivations, but also to begin to look for sources of judgment and shame. Clients often have internalized cultural and social sex-negative messaging that will bubble up when you discuss their reactions to this activity. Take care to notice any judgment coming from one partner to another. Make sure to highlight the sources of shame. Where did your clients learn that one motivation for sex is bad while another is good? Test the reality of these beliefs and assumptions with your clients, making sure to emphasize that these attitudes and assumptions were learned from their environment and aren't necessarily true.

It is important to note that designating a motivation as "good" or "bad" involves making a judgment about that particular motivation. Later, your clients will come to understand the large role that shame plays in sabotaging their sexual well-being. The first step in dismantling that shame is identifying it when it creeps in. Making good or bad judgments about motivations for sex, or even particular sexual behaviors, reinforces and promotes that shame.

Take time to educate your clients about the benefits of sex. While our sex-negative culture suggests that there are better and worse reasons for pursuing sex, we can bypass these judgments by focusing on what needs are being met by pursuing sexual activity. If your clients are feeling shame around any particular result from sexual activity (e.g., stress relief, closeness, soothing), reframe these motivations as attempts to get something that they need. Perhaps one of your clients pursues sex when they're feeling insecure in their relationship. Sex does indeed foster feelings of intimacy and security—mission accomplished! It is up to your clients whether they want to achieve security by pursuing sex or by other means, but it is not shameful to desire security in one's relationship. For each sex motivation that induces shame, help your clients identify the needs they are trying to meet, and have an open, nonjudgmental conversation about whether or not they want to continue to meet that particular need through sexual behavior.

To start such conversations, think about posing something like this:

Rather than framing particular motivations as good or bad, consider the following questions: Is this motivation likely to enhance or detract from my relationship with myself and with my partner? Does this motivation allow for the consent and sexual autonomy of my partner and the people impacted by my sexual behavior? Is satisfying this motivation actually within my control, or does it require others for me to react or feel a particular way? The answers to these questions are much more likely to provide you with a nonjudgmental understanding of how sex has functioned for you in the past, and how you may like it to function in the future. Take some time to talk to your partner. How would each person like sex to function in this relationship?

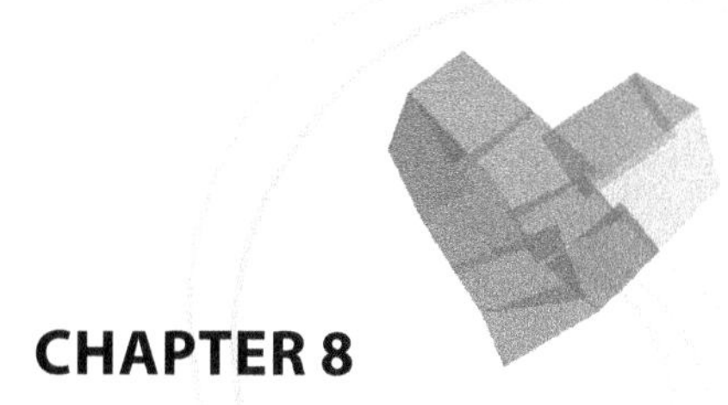

CHAPTER 8

Desire and Arousal

In chapter 7, you learned about some of the benefits of and motivations for sexual behavior. So, if sex is so important, why can it be so difficult to understand? In this chapter, you will learn about two of the more complicated processes related to sex: desire and arousal. When you understand the intricacies of desire and arousal, you will be better equipped to understand how your clients operate as sexual beings.

When it comes to partnered sex, there will always be discrepancies in desire and arousal. Perhaps one partner wants more sex than the other. Or perhaps one partner wanted to engage in something that was arousing to them but not to the other—or vice versa. This chapter will help you understand why such discrepancies occur and reduce shame around your clients' (and your own) sexuality so that you may help them manage these differences much more easily.

Arousal versus Desire

First, it should be noted that there is much discussion around what exactly is the difference, if any, between desire and arousal. For the purposes of this book, we will use the following definitions: *Arousal* can refer to both what our bodies are doing (e.g., engorgement or lubrication of the genitals) and what our minds are doing (e.g., thinking about sex or our partner). *Desire* refers to the subjective experience of wanting to engage in sexual behavior. In short, we can think of arousal as a physiological and cognitive process, while desire is a subjective, emotional experience. That said, it is likely that arousal and desire reinforce one another; in other words, they are related to and influence one another.

Arousal

There are two types of arousal: physiological and psychological. *Physiological arousal* is our bodies' response to sexually relevant information. Signs of physiological arousal include increased blood flow to erectile tissue in the penis, clitoris, and labia; increased sensitivity in genital and erogenous zones; and lubrication and elongation of the vagina.

Psychological arousal is a bit more complicated. According to the dual-control model of psychological arousal (Bancroft et al., 2009), there are two distinct yet related systems in the brain: the sexual excitation system (SES) and the sexual inhibition system (SIS). These two systems operate simultaneously and independently. In brief, the SES scans the environment for prosexual information, while the SIS scans the environment for antisexual information. Emily Nagoski (2015), a leading sex researcher and author, likens these systems to the gas pedal (SES) and brake pedal (SIS) on a car. For each individual, like each car, the gas and brake have different sensitivities. For example, someone with a sensitive gas pedal requires little psychological stimulation to be interested in sex, whereas someone with a not-so-sensitive gas pedal requires much more stimulation to be interested in sex. Similarly, a sensitive brake means a person may be easily influenced by many factors that inhibit arousal, while an insensitive brake may require strong inhibition to dampen sexual interest.

To make matters even more complicated, because psychological and physiological arousal are separate processes, they don't always occur together. Having them occur together—a phenomenon known as *concordant arousal*—is what many think of as a "normal" sexual experience. However, it's just as "normal" for the opposite to occur. Have you ever had an experience during which you thought you wanted to be sexual, but your body didn't cooperate? Or perhaps your body was responding when your brain wasn't really interested? These phenomena are called *discordant arousal*, and they are very, very common. Moreover, levels of arousal fluctuate across time. Sometimes arousal fluctuates over a matter of hours or days; sometimes it happens over weeks, months, or even years. This is because our internal and external environments are subject to change, and with those changes, different things press on our gas and brake pedals.

Desire

The subjective experience of wanting to have sex is, by definition, different for different people. Because people have varying sensitivities of their gas and brake pedals, and because the context or environment influences desire, we experience desire differently. The types of desire depend on what happens when stimulation is introduced.

Spontaneous Desire

Spontaneous desire occurs when someone experiences desire almost immediately after stimulation occurs. People with highly sensitive gas pedals are likely to experience spontaneous desire. In addition, people who are in an environment that primes them for sexual excitement are more likely to experience desire as spontaneous. For example, perhaps you've been sending flirty texts all day, and your partner finally comes home and kisses you passionately. Desire is likely to occur so quickly that it feels spontaneous.

Responsive Desire

Responsive desire occurs when there is a delay between stimulation and desire. Perhaps you have had a pleasant, albeit not particularly sexy day and haven't had a single thought about sex. Your partner comes home and kisses you passionately; you, experiencing pleasure from that kiss, begin to think about whether or not you may want to be sexual. Depending on the context, the answer to that question may be yes or no. When the answer is yes, you've experienced responsive desire. Those who have moderately to highly sensitive brake pedals are more likely to experience responsive desire.

To recap: Psychological arousal is the result of the interaction between our gas and brake. Physiological arousal is how our bodies respond to sexually relevant information. Both psychological and physiological arousal can result in and influence desire—that is, motivation for sexual behavior.

Sexual Mythbusting

Now that we've covered the basic factors in sexual behavior, let's look at some of the common myths around desire and arousal. You may recall that sexuality is influenced by biopsychosocial factors. Beliefs about how desire works, or should work, are formed primarily by social factors. Specifically, myths around desire are often the product of inaccurate cultural messaging and a lack of adequate, sex-positive education. It is likely that your clients will come in with some of these erroneous beliefs. To enable you to gently correct them, we've provided you with some of the most common myths—and the facts that refute them.

It is worth noting that cultural myths around sex tend to be based on gender stereotypes. In addition, trans, genderfluid, and nonbinary people (as well as other marginalized groups, such as people of color) are underrepresented in sex research studies and literature on the subject. For simplicity's sake, we have used the terms "man" and "woman" in the following table, but those terms do not limit the application of these myths and facts to cisgender men and women exclusively.

Myth	Fact
Libido (the desire to have sex) is a biological drive/need that must be met.	Sex is a motivated behavior. A biological drive is a behavior that is necessary for survival (e.g., hunger, thirst).

Myth	Fact
Men have a higher libido than women.	There is no evidence to suggest that there are significant differences between levels of desire in men and women.
All men have a high sex drive.	Research suggests that there is as much variability in levels of sexual desire among men as there is among women.
If a man has an erection, he wants to have sex; if a woman is self-lubricating, she wants to have sex.	Physiological arousal only indicates that the body is responding to sexually relevant information. It is not the same as psychological arousal, which is also necessary for consensual sex.
It is impossible to be confused about whether or not you want to have sex.	It is possible to be psychologically or physiologically aroused independent of the other.
Your partner's level of desire reflects their level of attraction or love for you.	A person's level of desire is reflective of the inputs of their SES, SIS, and pleasurable stimuli. In this framework, a person's arousal is about what that person is experiencing, not a reflection of their partner.
You can't increase your sex drive.	You can increase your levels of interest and desire by harnessing information about your turn-ons and turn-offs, and by creating contexts that promote sexual expression and pleasure.
A satisfying sex life requires strong desire.	What is "satisfying" for one person is determined by that person alone. Those with lower levels of desire can have perfectly satisfying sex lives, depending on what "satisfying" means to them.

Myth	Fact
You need to have a lot of sex to maintain a high sex drive.	While it is true that having sex can lead to having more sex, a person's level of desire is highly contextual, and previous sexual experience is just one of the many factors that influence desire.
Having low sexual desire means that you don't enjoy sex.	People with lower levels of desire do enjoy sex! They just don't experience wanting sex as often as those with higher levels of desire.
Sexual desire should be spontaneous.	Sexual desire is highly contextual. You may not realize it, but your brain and body are constantly reacting and adjusting to the environment around you. In fact, what you may experience as spontaneous desire is likely a response to the various stimuli around you.

Educate your clients on arousal and desire. In particular, make sure that they understand the dual-control model, discordant arousal, and the importance of the environment in desire, as these concepts will be foundational for work to come. The following activity is helpful in informing clients about their own gas and brake pedals.

Client Activity

Sexual Temperament Questionnaire*

Sexual Inhibitory System (SIS)

Unless things are "just right," it is difficult for me to become sexually aroused.

0	1	2	3	4
Not at all like me	Not much like me	Somewhat like me	A lot like me	Exactly like me

When I am sexually aroused, the slightest thing can turn me off.

0	1	2	3	4
Not at all like me	Not much like me	Somewhat like me	A lot like me	Exactly like me

I have to trust a partner to become fully aroused.

0	1	2	3	4
Not at all like me	Not much like me	Somewhat like me	A lot like me	Exactly like me

If I am worried about taking too long to become aroused or to orgasm, this can interfere with my arousal.

0	1	2	3	4
Not at all like me	Not much like me	Somewhat like me	A lot like me	Exactly like me

Sometimes I feel so "shy" or self-conscious during sex that I cannot become fully aroused.

0	1	2	3	4
Not at all like me	Not much like me	Somewhat like me	A lot like me	Exactly like me

Total: ______

* This questionnaire and its accompanying scoring key are adapted with permission from *Come As You Are: The Surprising New Science of Women's Sexual Wellbeing* (pp. 54–57), by E. Nagoski, 2015, Simon & Schuster.

Sexual Excitatory System (SES)

Often just how someone smells can be a turn-on.

0	1	2	3	4
Not at all like me	Not much like me	Somewhat like me	A lot like me	Exactly like me

Seeing a partner doing something that shows their talent or intelligence, or watching them interacting well with others can make me very sexually aroused.

0	1	2	3	4
Not at all like me	Not much like me	Somewhat like me	A lot like me	Exactly like me

Having sex in a different setting than usual is a real turn-on for me.

0	1	2	3	4
Not at all like me	Not much like me	Somewhat like me	A lot like me	Exactly like me

When I think about someone I find sexually attractive or fantasize about sex, I easily become sexually aroused.

0	1	2	3	4
Not at all like me	Not much like me	Somewhat like me	A lot like me	Exactly like me

Certain hormonal changes definitely increase my sexual arousal.

0	1	2	3	4
Not at all like me	Not much like me	Somewhat like me	A lot like me	Exactly like me

I get very turned on when someone wants me sexually.

0	1	2	3	4
Not at all like me	Not much like me	Somewhat like me	A lot like me	Exactly like me

Total: ______

Low SIS (0–6)

You're not so sensitive to all the reasons not to be sexually aroused. You don't tend to worry about your own sexual functioning, and body image issues don't interfere too much with your sexuality. When you're sexually engaged, your attention is not very distractible, and you wouldn't be inclined to describe yourself as "sexually shy." Most circumstances can be sexual for you. You may find that your main challenge around sexual functioning is holding yourself back, reining yourself in. Staying aware of potential consequences can help with this.

Medium SIS (7–13)

You're right in the middle. This means that whether or not your sexual "brakes" engage will be largely dependent on context. Risky or novel situations, such as a new partner, might increase your concerns about your own sexual functioning, your shyness, or your distractibility during sex. Contexts that easily arouse you are likely to be low risk and more familiar, and anytime your stress escalates—including anxiety, depression, overwhelm, and exhaustion—your brakes will reduce your interest in and response to sexual signals.

High SIS (14–20)

You're pretty sensitive to all the reasons not to be sexually aroused. You need a setting of trust and relaxation in order to be aroused, and it's best if you don't feel rushed or pressured in any way. You might be easily distracted from sex. High SIS, regardless of SES, is the most strongly correlated factor with sexual problems.

Low SES (0–6)

You're not so sensitive to sex-related stimuli and need to make a more deliberate effort to tune your attention in that direction. Novel situations are less likely to be sexy to you than familiar ones. You're a person whose sexual functioning will benefit from adding a greater intensity of stimulation (like a vibrator) and daily practice of paying attention to sensations. Lower SES is also associated with asexuality, so if you're very low SE, you might resonate with some components of the asexual identity.

Medium SES (7–13)

You're right in the middle, so whether or not you're sensitive to sexual stimuli probably depends on the context. In situations of high romance or eroticism, you tune in readily to sexual stimuli; and in situations of low romance or eroticism, it may be pretty challenging to move your attention to sexual things. Recognize the role that context plays in your arousal and pleasure, and take steps to increase the sexiness of your life's contexts.

High SES (14–20)

You're pretty sensitive to sex-related stimuli, maybe even to things humans aren't generally very sensitive to, like smell and taste. A fairly wide range of contexts can be sexual for you, and novelty may be really exciting. You may be a person who likes having sex as a way to de-stress. Your sexual functioning may benefit from making sure you create lots of time and space for your partner; because you're sensitive, you can derive intense satisfaction from your partner's pleasure, so you'll both benefit!

Sexual Temperament Questionnaire Debrief

Explore your clients' results with them. Notice their reactions to their results and the results of their partner. Often people on the extremes, particularly those with high SIS, pathologize themselves. They label themselves or get labeled by their partner as "the problem" in their shared sex life. This is an excellent time to remind your clients that their results are just information, not a diagnosis. If someone's results are toward the extremes, that's okay. They are here to gather information about their sexuality and harness that information to create a sex life that feels good to them. Remember, the gas and brake pedals are just some of the variables involved in sexual desire. Take this as an opportunity to remind your clients about the importance of the environment in which sexual behavior occurs. In addition, you may want to remind them of the framework for treatment (the couple versus the problem) as well as their definition of success.

Dealing with Discrepancies Between Partners

If your clients complete the sexual temperament questionnaire and find discrepancies in their individual sexual temperaments, they may take this as a sign that they are fundamentally incompatible or that the relationship is doomed. Assure them that there is no need to panic. Differences in sexual temperament do indeed pose a problem, but it is not an unsolvable one. The solution is as simple in concept as it is challenging to implement. Think of the three components of desire: gas pedal, brake pedal, and environment. Increasing desire is a matter of understanding what activates each of these systems and actively encouraging environmental factors that promote desire.

The following activity will help your clients understand more about how the environment in which sex occurs can influence their levels of desire and arousal.

Client Activity

Sexual Environment

Think about one of your most positive sexual experiences. Write down what factors were present or made it positive. Now, think of a less positive sexual experience, and list the factors that contributed to it being less than positive. Use the prompts in the chart below to help stimulate your thinking.

Category	Positive	Less Positive
During this sexual experience, how were you feeling mentally? • How was your mood? ◦ Were you distracted? ◦ Worried about sexual functioning? ◦ Anxious about your partner's pleasure?		
How were you feeling physically? • How were you feeling about your body? • Your health? • Your hygiene?		

What did you notice about your partner? • How were you feeling about their physical appearance? • Their health? • Their hygiene? • Their mental state?		
How were you feeling about your relationship? • How emotionally connected did you feel? • How satisfied were you with the sexual relationship overall? • Did power dynamics play a role in how you felt? If so, how? • How much trust were you feeling in the relationship?		
What was the setting like? • Was it in public or private? • At home or elsewhere? • In person or at a distance? • Were you inspired by something that your partner did?		
What were your stress levels like? • Regarding work? • Regarding finances? • Regarding family? • Regarding your interpersonal dynamic?		

Were there special circumstances? • Was it during a holiday/vacation? • Was it on an anniversary/birthday? • Was it an unexpected opportunity?		
What kinds of mental stimulation were present? • Internal fantasy? • External fantasy (e.g., dirty talk or role-play)? • Power dynamics? • Kink fulfillment? • Novelty?		
What kinds of physical stimulation were present? • Erogenous foreplay? • Received/provided oral/digital stimulation? • Intercourse? • Props? • Toys?		
Other relevant factors		

Sexual Environment Debrief

Have your clients review their answers from the *Sexual Environment* activity. Go over the information in the positive sexual experience column. Which of the factors that they wrote down might be real turn-ons for them? Now take a look at the less positive experience column. Do they notice any turn-offs? Have your clients circle the factors in each column that really make a difference for them, and make sure each partner shares this with the other.

As you can see, desire and arousal are not just about sexual behavior. Both processes are affected by how we feel physically, emotionally, and relationally. Even our external environment can affect our levels of desire and arousal. These factors are far more likely to be causes of change in desire than permanent changes in libido or physical attractiveness.

CHAPTER 9

Sexual Communication

So far, you've learned why sex is important, and you've got a good understanding of how people experience desire and arousal. Hopefully, you've been able to determine why sex might be important to your clients, and you've developed an understanding of the biopsychosocial factors that promote and inhibit positive sexual experiences for each of them specifically.

As you have read time and time again, discrepancies between partners' sexualities are the rule, not the exception. Sexuality is multifaceted and specific to the individual. When someone participates in a partnered sexual interaction, they have to deal with the individual needs and preferences of each person involved. No wonder it doesn't always match up! Moreover, anytime you are working with individual preferences and needs, you are likely to encounter two difficult hurdles: conflict and shame. Conflict is likely to arise whenever you are dealing with two people in two different bodies, simply because each person may want different things that cannot be satisfied at the same time. Shame is a deep vulnerability that we all deal with, especially when it comes to sex. Because most of us are steeped in sex negativity throughout our lives, we become very concerned about whether or not our wants and needs are acceptable. The bad news is that conflict and shame often derail communication between partners pretty quickly. But there is good news, as well. If your clients experience conflict in their sexual relationship, this is an indicator that they're trying to be honest with each other. It's actually a marker of a positive relationship, not an indication that something is wrong. You've already learned how to help your clients overcome conflict; now you're going to learn how to help them overcome shame. Begin by having them complete the following two-part activity on improving their sexual communication.

Client Activity

Sexual Communication, Part A

There are two parts to this activity. First, you are going to look at your general feelings about sexual communication in your relationships. Then, you will explore a specific instance of sexual communication.

Part A: The Dyadic Sexual Communication Scale* helps elucidate areas of strength and weakness in partners' sexual communication. Please note that this measure was developed using two-person relationships. To ensure valid results, if you are involved in multiple relationships simultaneously, choose one in which sexual communication could be improved.

As you read each statement, indicate how much you agree or disagree with it, with 1 being "disagree strongly and 6 being "agree strongly."

	1 Disagree Strongly	2	3	4	5	6 Agree Strongly
1. My partner rarely responds when I want to talk about our sex life.	☐	☐	☐	☐	☐	☐
2. Some sexual matters are too upsetting to discuss with my sexual partner.	☐	☐	☐	☐	☐	☐
3. There are sexual issues or problems in our sexual relationship that we have never discussed.	☐	☐	☐	☐	☐	☐
4. My partner and I never seem to resolve our disagreements about sexual matters.	☐	☐	☐	☐	☐	☐

* This scale is reproduced with permission from "Dyadic Sexual Communication Scale," in R. R. Milhausen, J. K. Sakaluk, T. D. Fisher, C. M. Davis, and W. L. Yarber (Eds.), *Handbook of Sexuality-Related Measures*, 4th ed. (pp. 212–214), by J. A. Catania, 2020, Routledge.

5. Whenever my partner and I talk about sex, I feel like they are lecturing me.	☐	☐	☐	☐	☐	☐
6. My partner often complains that I am not very clear about what I want sexually.	☐	☐	☐	☐	☐	☐
7. My partner and I have never had a heart-to-heart talk about our sex life together.	☐	☐	☐	☐	☐	☐
8. My partner has no difficulty in talking to me about their sexual feelings and desires.	☐	☐	☐	☐	☐	☐
9. Even when angry with me, my partner is able to appreciate my views on sexuality.	☐	☐	☐	☐	☐	☐
10. Talking about sex is a satisfying experience for both of us.	☐	☐	☐	☐	☐	☐
11. My partner and I can usually talk calmly about our sex life.	☐	☐	☐	☐	☐	☐
12. I have little difficulty telling my partner what I do or don't do sexually.	☐	☐	☐	☐	☐	☐
13. I seldom feel embarrassed when talking about the details of our sex life with my partner.	☐	☐	☐	☐	☐	☐

Take a look at your responses. Are you more likely to endorse items that indicate that it is difficult for you to discuss sex with partners, or do your answers indicate you are comfortable discussing sex? How do your results compare to that of your partner? If one of you feels more comfortable talking about sex than the other, lean on them for support in your future conversations. Their comfort can help instill confidence in you.

Sexual Communication, Part A Debrief

First, compare your clients' results to one another. Are they on the same page? Or does one partner think that their communication is much better or worse than the other? Is there embarrassment at speaking their preferences aloud? Conflict from not knowing how to address differences between them and their partner? Difficulty being truly honest and forthcoming? A lack of responsiveness toward one another? Emotionality during the conversations? Looking at the areas in which your clients' *do not* match up is a good start to identifying the barriers to communication that they face.

Barriers to Communication

Despite our good intentions and best efforts, even the best relationships can suffer from barriers to productive communication. Common barriers include disconnection from the body, lack of knowledge, embarrassment, and guilt.

Disconnection from the Body

Disconnection from the body is a fancy way of saying that sometimes we don't attend to or know what our bodies are feeling. If clients don't know how their bodies feel, it is almost impossible to describe what they want. First, make sure that they have the language they need to describe their anatomy. Second, suggest that your client, either with their partner or alone, experiment with different kinds of touch and describe out loud how they feel. Ask them to note what feels pleasurable: Are there specific types of touch or specific places that feel better than others? Encourage your client to share this information with their partner.

For some people, connecting to the body can feel impossible or even dangerous. If your client dissociates or is not ready to experience touch while staying present in their body, that is okay. Simply back up and help them feel grounded in their body without touch. Grounding exercises, progressive muscle relaxation, and mindfulness meditation can be helpful tools to make it safe to be connected to the body. Once safety is established, then you can move on to touch.

Lack of Knowledge

Lack of knowledge is another barrier to communication. Like being disconnected from the body, not knowing what possibilities might be out there makes it very difficult to explore what your clients might want. Talk with them to assess their level of knowledge about their bodies, their partners' bodies, and common types of sexual stimulation. Explore their experiences and help them identify pathways toward increased pleasure. You may also educate them on common anatomy using clinical language, noting both genital and non-genital erogenous zones.

Embarrassment

Embarrassment is a common experience when talking about sex. It is incredibly vulnerable to be open and honest about our desires and fantasies. It can be helpful to first label the embarrassment and normalize it. In addition, you may offer examples of fantasies, ranging from the common to the less common; this can help your clients become more comfortable with the wide-ranging world of sexual desire. Helping your clients understand how vast the sexual landscape can be may help them understand that their desires and fantasies are not as uncommon as they might think.

In addition, many clients aren't used to using explicit clinical language to discuss their bodies and sexual desires. Model this type of language when offering examples of things that people may find sexually interesting.

Guilt

Guilt often arises when people try to talk about sex. Many clients will assume that talking about what they want will imply that their partner is lacking (whether real or imagined) in some way. First, assess whether or not this is true. If the partner feels that they are letting their partner down, remind them that they should not just magically know what their partner wants. They are not in their partner's body, so they cannot know unless their partner tells them. Furthermore, each partner is responsible for telling the other what they want. It is no one's job to intuit or mind read the other partner's desires.

Client Activity

Sexual Communication, Part B

Think about a specific instance when you and your partner had a conversation about sex that didn't go as planned. Write down your answers to the following questions, then talk with your partner and identify one or two aspects of your communication that you want to improve.

How did you feel at the beginning of the conversation?	
What was happening when the conversation took a turn?	
How did you leave the conversation (e.g., did you feel connected, withdrawn, angry)?	
What did you feel afterward?	

Were you able to get what you wanted out of the conversation?	
What did your partner do or say that was helpful?	
What did your partner do or say that was hurtful?	
What do you wish you had done differently?	

Sexual Communication, Part B Debrief

Have one client share their experience of a conversation. Their partner's job is simply to listen without responding, defending themselves, or deflecting. Help your clients understand where the conversation went off the rails and what may have triggered them. Develop a strategy with them to help keep the conversation on track the next time. Then let the other client share the conversation they have chosen to document, repeating the same steps.

Why Is This So Hard?

Communicating about sex is often a difficult—and at times seemingly impossible—task. It can bring up feelings of shame, inadequacy, fear, and even anger. Many partners enter discussions about their sex lives only to leave the conversation feeling defeated and disconnected. As mentioned in the beginning of the chapter, the conflict and shame we feel about our sexual desires and history can make communicating about sex difficult.

Conflict

As you have already learned, the presence of conflict is not necessarily bad. In fact, conflict is inevitable when two or more people share experiences together, simply because we are all different people with different wants and needs. You may want to revisit the previous chapters on conflict and conflict resolution to refresh that information if needed.

There are a few additional points to keep in mind when you see your clients experiencing conflict around sexual issues. First, most people feel discomfort talking about sex, so be kind. Second, your clients' sexual desires do not have to match perfectly in order for them to have a sexually satisfying relationship. Third, your clients are not responsible for meeting their partner's every sexual want or need. Lastly, adhere to the golden rule of talking about sex: *do not yuck someone else's yum.* (Note: this rule does not apply to sexually abusive behaviors.) If a client is not into something, that's okay! Just because something holds erotic value for one person doesn't mean it holds erotic value for another. However, everyone is vulnerable and prone to shame when talking about sex. Think of how you would feel if someone yucked your yum. You don't want that to happen to you; don't do it to your clients or allow them to do it to one another. There is no right for everyone; there is only right for each individual person.

Shame

Despite the fact that sexual behavior is incredibly common among humans, we are often afraid to talk about it for fear of judgment or rejection. Even when we intellectually know that we don't deserve judgment or rejection, the fear of it creates the internal feeling that we do, in fact, somehow deserve it. What makes such a common part of life so scary? The biggest factors contributing to the shame that most people feel around sex are sex negativity and a lack of adequate sexual education.

As we discussed back in chapter 1, the environment around us, such as our family beliefs and behaviors, cultural attitudes, and media portrayal, affect our opinions and beliefs around sex, often without us realizing it. And most often, we are exposed to negative and conflicting messages around sex. These messages begin from a very young age and shape our beliefs and attitudes toward sex. Nagoski (2015) uses a garden metaphor to describe the impact of these insidious forces. Think of your understanding of sex and sexuality as a garden plot. Before you can even speak, let alone form your own opinions, the people, culture, and media around you are planting the seeds of assumptions and preconceived notions in that garden. While it's possible that these seeds could yield beautiful sunflowers, the prevailing attitude toward sex in our culture makes it far more likely that they will produce weeds.

Later in life, you stumble upon this garden, perhaps when sexuality becomes a more present force in your life. Like most people, you see a plot full of weeds and accept them as the only possible plants in that garden because no one ever told you that there could be sunflowers. Not sure that you love those weeds? Too bad—there are no other options; furthermore, you've been sworn to secrecy about the contents of your garden because you have been taught not to discuss issues of sex and sexuality with anyone else.

While some families, communities, and cultures regard these weeds as necessary measures to protect young people from dangers they associate with sex, there are many others who unintentionally plant weeds by relying on the "sex education" offered in school or through other community institutions. The assumption is that this instruction will be largely neutral given that it focuses primarily on reproductive health: anatomy, the changes in bodies during puberty, and the basics of fertilization and gestation. The discussion of actual sex mostly involves warning against the dangers of STIs, unwanted pregnancy, and moral failing. In other words, weeds, weeds, and more weeds. Of course, reproductive health is important, but it is not *sexual* health. Unless someone's "sexual education" included accurate information about the risks of different types of sexual behavior (without scare tactics), the importance of pleasure, and how to give and receive consent, it was not real sex education. Real sex education results in a garden full of sunflowers.

Sex Negativity Sabotages Sexual Communication

Being able to talk about sex is a huge step toward helping your clients weed out their garden and plant sunflowers. Like many important things, it is also difficult. One of the most destructive and invasive weeds that we encounter is *sexual shame*. It comes in many forms. Perhaps your clients have experienced shame over the presence, content, or frequency of their desire or the way their body does or does not react in sexual situations. Perhaps they feel pressure to look a certain way, feel a certain way, or participate in a certain kind of behavior because they believe it's expected. Perhaps they've pretended to be more comfortable or knowledgeable about something than they actually were at the time. The list of possibilities for sexuality-related shame is endless.

When clients try to talk to their partner about sex, all this shame can rise to the surface. They have been taught that they should be ashamed of these things, so it is an enormous risk to reveal them to you and their partner. What is worse than growing a shame weed? Having it confirmed through the judgment and rejection of a person they trust. Perhaps your clients avoid these conversations for fear that they will be shamed, or perhaps they have been so vague as to not say what they actually wanted to say. This is why the golden rule is golden. If your clients are open to having productive conversation with a partner around sex, they have to trust that you and their partner will not yuck their yum.

Guidelines for Sexual Communication

Before you read the guidelines, it is important to understand the principles on which they are based. As you have seen in previous chapters, the tenets of conflict resolution inform these guidelines. The other important concept is sex positivity. Explanations and definitions of sex positivity vary, but there are core attributes that are shared by most models. In short, a stance of sex positivity involves holding and cultivating positive attitudes toward sex, being interested in exploring sexuality, being open and nonjudgmental toward the interests of others even when they are not your particular interest, and affirming a practice of consent. In other words, a person practicing sex positivity is interested in understanding and defining sexual pleasure and satisfaction for themselves and is concerned with others—especially their partner—understanding this for themselves.

Now, on to what you are really here for: the nuts and bolts of improving your ability to teach your clients how to discuss sex and sexuality with their partner. These are general guidelines for communicating around sex (we'll get to more specific scenarios in the next chapter). Remember, sex is about pleasure, intimacy, connection, and exploration. In other words, good things. Shame and anxiety will tell your clients that conversations around sex are treacherous and fraught. In reality, conversations surrounding sex are simply to improve and build upon a positive aspect of their relationship. To the extent possible, approach such discussions as opportunities to strengthen their bond. Also, keep in mind that many conversations about sex and sexuality are ongoing or made of several parts. Remind your clients not to pressure themselves to wrap it all up in a neat little bow the first time they discuss something.

The following handout includes the guidelines for sexual communication. Familiarize yourself with them so that you can teach your clients how to communicate effectively and respectfully.

Client Handout

Guidelines for Sexual Communication

1. **Ask for permission. Obtain consent.** As you have learned over the work you have done so far, talking about sex can be challenging and emotionally laborious. Just because you are ready to dive into a conversation does not mean that someone else is. Before jumping into the content of what you want to say, check to see if your partner has the bandwidth to listen and respond.

2. **Be honest. Be explicit.** If you're going to do the work of talking about sex, make sure you get to say what you need to say. Vague language will sabotage any sexual conversation. Make sure the person that you're talking to knows what you're saying by asking for their understanding and clarifying any miscommunications.
3. **Use I-statements.** This is a good rule to follow for any emotional conversation—or any conversation, really! I-statements allow you to take responsibility for how you feel and help you avoid the pitfall of blaming your feelings on someone else's behavior. This helps everyone involved stay open and empathic during the conversation. For example, "I'm worried that I may not be desirable to you anymore" is a much more inviting statement than "You're not attracted to me anymore." The first statement expresses your own experience and allows room for reassurance. The second statement accuses your partner of doing something wrong, and it is likely to result in defensiveness or combativeness.
4. **Expect differences.** You and whoever you're talking to are different people. Your interests, desires, and boundaries are going to be different (hopefully with some overlap). Differences are not necessarily problems. In fact, nothing is an inherent problem unless you or your partner are negatively impacted by that particular thing.
5. **Follow the golden rule.** If you only take one thing from these guidelines, let this be it. You do not have to like or be interested in everything that your partner may be interested in. You do, however, have to respect and affirm their desire. *Do not yuck their yum*. If you are turned off by someone else's desire, don't worry. It's just not for you, but it can still be great for them.
6. **Make a plan for reconnection.** Despite our best efforts to facilitate open, constructive dialogue, discussing sexual matters can be emotionally difficult. While these guidelines are important, they are not a fail-safe against others becoming upset. Have

a plan for how you and your partner will reconnect if the conversation does go awry. Perhaps you share a genuine hug or do a nonsexual activity that you both enjoy. Be creative and develop a way to reconnect that works for your relationship.

Client Activity

Implementing Guidelines

Revisit the interaction that you wrote about in the *Sexual Communication, Part B* activity. In the following list of sexual communication guidelines, place a check mark by the ones you employed in this interaction.

Sexual Communication Guidelines

- ☐ Ask for permission. Obtain consent.
- ☐ Be honest. Be explicit.
- ☐ Use I-statements.
- ☐ Expect differences.
- ☐ Follow the golden rule. (Do not yuck someone else's yum.)
- ☐ Make a plan for reconnection.

Now note which of the guidelines you didn't employ in this interaction. If you'd been following these guidelines, how might the conversations have been different? How would your answers to the questions change?

Implementing Guidelines Debrief

Help your clients restart the conversations from the *Sexual Communication, Part B* activity, and gently remind them of the guidelines when they go astray. It is not necessary that they finish the conversation, just that they have the experience of having a contained, calm exchange of ideas and information.

Client Activity

Creating Sexual Goals

The following questions will get you thinking about aspects of your sexual relationship that you might want to change or improve. Use your answers to create one or more goals toward improving your sexual relationship. When you are finished, share your goal(s) with your partner.

Do you feel anxious when you think about your sexual relationship?

____

____

____

How do you feel about the kind of sex that you are having or not having?

____

____

____

Is there something about your sex life that feels uncomfortable, upsetting, or stressful?

____

____

____

Which things do you wish you could tell your partner about what you like or don't like?

____

____

____

What might you like to try with your partner?

____

____

____

Safety and Consent

Step one of any sexual exploration is always safety. Most people think about safety as physical. Of course, it is important to make sure that any sexual activity that could cause physical injury is as safe as possible. However, we must also consider *psychological safety*. Psychological safety is the belief that we will not be punished, humiliated, or shamed for discussing our ideas, feelings, concerns, and questions. It is the expectation that our ideas, feelings, concerns, and questions will be met with acceptance, affirmation, and respect. Establishing and maintaining psychological safety begins with true consent.

What Is Consent?

Consent is an agreement between two or more people to engage in a sexual activity. In order for consent to be trusted, it must meet certain criteria. Consent must be given freely (i.e., not coerced) and must be able to be withdrawn at any time without consequence. It is an ongoing process, meaning that an affirmative response to one activity is not an affirmative response for other activities or activities in the future. Furthermore, all participants must be able to communicate clearly and coherently. It may be important for your clients to have conversations about sex before they are in a sexual situation, particularly if they have a tendency to feel pressure or anxiety. Help your clients discuss how to communicate consent or lack thereof during a sexual encounter. For instance, they may consent to sexual activity that restricts a participant's abilities to speak or see; it is vital in this instance that you help them strategize and agree to alternate forms of communication. It is also important to help your clients develop a plan for what to do when consent is not given or withdrawn. This can be a disconnecting and jarring experience, and you want to help your clients maintain their connection as much as possible.

Sometimes, it can be easier to conceptualize what consent *isn't*. Consent is not an affirmative response resulting from coercion or persuasion. Consent is not the absence of a no or a protest. Consent cannot be given by vulnerable or incapacitated people (e.g., children, intoxicated persons, sleeping persons, unconscious persons).

Why Is Consent Important?

To maintain an open and trusting sexual relationship, participants must be able to communicate freely without fear of judgment, rejection, or punishment. Importantly, consent is a loving and respectful process. When participating in sexual experiences with others, we demonstrate care by paying attention to what our partners want and what they do not want. Also, sex is much more enjoyable if people aren't worrying about whether or not things are okay!

Not only is it important to actively ask for consent, but it is also important to be able to deny consent. Often, people are afraid to say no to sexual activity for fear of disappointing their partner; however, this undermines trust. We cannot trust a yes if we never hear a no. It is just as important to respond truthfully as it is to ask for consent.

Sexual behavior without consent is both abusive and criminal. If someone performs sexual acts on or in the presence of a person who did not consent to that act, they are, in fact, assaulting that person. It is abusive to behave without consent, and it is also abusive to impose consequences on someone when they deny consent. For example, becoming angry with a partner and withdrawing warmth and affection after they set a boundary is a form of punishment and therefore abuse. If someone creates an environment that is physically or psychologically threatening for their partner to say no, they have created a toxic and abusive environment.

Many people have fantasies and interests that are directly related to a lack of consent. When engaging in sexual activity that hinges on the absence of consent, an element of role-play is necessary. Your clients should discuss boundaries and desires with their partner ahead of time, consenting to behaviors then. This keeps the fantasy alive during the experience. Make sure that they also discuss ahead of time how to communicate ongoing consent, distress, or the withdrawal of consent during the interaction.

Make sure that your clients fully understand what consent is and is not before moving on.

Common Conversations

In previous chapters, you learned about how to converse with your clients about sex and sexuality, including how to avoid the pitfalls that most people fall into when discussing sex. In this section, you will learn how to tackle specific issues that may be relevant to your clients' sexual relationships in the past, present, and future.

In the following pages, you will explore several common challenges that people face in their sexual relationships. Of course, the scenarios here are not exhaustive, and this section cannot cover every potential challenge. Some issues that people encounter are so complex, long-standing, or deeply ingrained that they simply cannot be explored in this format. Remember that you can always refer out when you encounter an issue with which you are unfamiliar.

When your clients begin to explore their sexual wants and desires, you are likely to encounter one or more of the following scenarios: expressing dissatisfaction, making or receiving a request, and setting or receiving a boundary.

When reviewing the following conversation examples, please keep in mind that any of these topics can be spread out over multiple discussions. In fact, should your clients become overwhelmed or flooded while discussing sex, it is best to take a break and revisit the conversation at another time.

Before continuing, remember the guidelines for sexual communication:

1. Ask for permission. Obtain consent.
2. Be honest. Be explicit.
3. Use "I-statements."
4. Expect differences.
5. Follow the golden rule. (Do not yuck someone else's yum.)
6. Make a plan for reconnection.

With these principles in mind, let's explore some common scenarios. For the following examples, you will be following a couple, Jessie and Alex, as they navigate their way through important conversations regarding their sex life together. Jessie and Alex have been together for three years, have been living together for a year, and are discussing marriage. Note that each scenario is independent of the previous scenarios.

Expressing Dissatisfaction

Anytime at least two people are involved in a sexual relationship, there will be conflict, and there will be some degree of dissatisfaction. If your clients want to improve their sexual well-being, they need to be able to talk about the areas of their sex lives that could use a bit of work. While it is unrealistic and unfair to expect their partners to meet all of their sexual desires, there is often much room for improvement if the couple begins a discussion of these issues together. Let's take a look at how Jessie and Alex navigate expressing dissatisfaction.

Since moving in together, the frequency and quality of Jessie and Alex's sex life have decreased. Jessie feels that they are not having sex often enough, and when they do, it feels routine. Alex seems unbothered by the change in their sex life. Since they started talking about marriage, Jessie begins to wonder if this is how their sex life will be forever and decides to address these issues with Alex.

Jessie is afraid to hurt Alex, afraid that things won't ever change, afraid that Alex is no longer interested, and afraid that this means they are sexually incompatible. What difficulties do you imagine might arise in their conversation? Based on the sexual communication guidelines, how might Jessie address these concerns with Alex?

Scenario A:

Jessie approaches Alex after they are both home from work. Alex had a challenging day and is grateful to just be home.

JESSIE: (*Having mustered up the courage*) I need to talk to you.

ALEX: (*Surprised*) What?

JESSIE: We don't have enough sex. And things aren't like they used to be.

ALEX: What? Yes we do. What do you mean?

JESSIE: It's like you don't even care anymore. Or don't want me. If this is how it's going to be, I'm not sure we should get married.

ALEX: Of course I care! We have a normal amount of sex. What are you even saying? If I don't put out more, you're going to leave me?

Analysis of Scenario A:

In scenario A, both Jessie and Alex made moves that contributed to the escalation of the conversation. First, Jessie opens with a statement containing an implicit demand, which startles Alex and increases the likelihood that Alex will be defensive. Furthermore, Jessie's opening does not allow any opportunity to determine whether or not Alex is ready to have an important conversation. Jessie then blurts out a version of the perceived conflict in a way that suggests something is wrong with both of them and the relationship, rather than taking accountability for their own feelings. Alex then gets defensive and attempts to argue Jessie's assertion that they don't have enough sex. In response, Jessie begins to make assumptions about Alex's feelings, then threatens the commitment to the relationship. In turn, Alex begins to get upset, catastrophizes, and implicitly accuses Jessie of being cruel. With each line, we see both Jessie and Alex using provocative language to which the other reacts strongly. They both begin to spiral and flood, moving further and further away from the issue at hand.

Scenario B:

JESSIE: (*Having mustered up the courage*) I'd like to talk to you about our sex life. Is now an okay time?

ALEX: (*Surprised*) Oh. Sure. What's going on?

JESSIE: I'm feeling worried about the change in how often and how we're having sex.

ALEX: Okay. What are you worried about?

JESSIE: I miss the sex that we used to have. I miss you, and I'm worried that the change means that I'm not desirable, or maybe that we're not sexually compatible?

ALEX: Of course not! I absolutely desire you. Listen, it has been a really long day. I agree that this is something that we need to talk more about. How about this weekend? I can think more about what you're saying, and we'll figure something out.

Analysis of Scenario B:

In scenario B, both Alex and Jessie make positive communication moves that allow them to have a constructive, rather than destructive, conversation. Jessie opens by asking whether or not Alex is available to discuss their sex life. This gives Alex the opportunity to consent to a conversation or request an alternate time to talk. Alex responds with curiosity rather than suspicion. Jessie, using an I-statement, clearly states how they are feeling without suggesting that Alex is to blame or requiring Alex to feel the same way. Instead of reacting to Jessie's concerns, Alex listens and again approaches Jessie with curiosity. Jessie explains more about how they are feeling, and they bring up the vulnerable worries that they have been attaching to the observations about their sex life. Rather than accusing Alex of not desiring or caring about them, Jessie simply states that the change in their sex life makes them worry about deeper issues. With this information, Alex can now address some of those deeper fears and comfort Jessie. Realizing that this conversation may require more emotional energy than Alex has at the end of a stressful day, Alex can lovingly suggest that they discuss this issue further during the weekend. This reassures Jessie that Alex understands the importance of their concerns and is committed to working through them, which allows Jessie to let the conversation go for now and wait until they can address their sexual challenges together.

Making or Receiving a Request

Making or receiving requests may follow conversations in which someone expresses dissatisfaction, or, for those more comfortable with sexual conflict, it may be a stand-alone conversation. Either way, both making and receiving requests can make us vulnerable to worries about compatibility, adequacy, attachment, and vulnerability. Again, we turn to Alex and Jessie as examples.

Since adolescence, Alex has been interested in exploring anal play with a partner. Embarrassed and worried about judgment and rejection, Alex has never told anyone. Wanting to be open and honest, Alex decides to tell Jessie.

When making a request, Alex should consider several questions. First, how important is exploring anal play to Alex's sexual satisfaction and well-being? It's good to have a sense of how deeply this conversation with Jessie may impact Alex.

Next, Alex should identify the important features of anal play. What about Alex's fantasy is the most meaningful? The most erotic? Asking and answering these questions will help Alex differentiate between wants and needs. Sexual needs are those things that are essential to our sexual well-being; wants are the ways that we try to meet those needs. For example, Alex may identify that at the core of their desire for anal play is actually a desire to share something novel and intimate with Jessie. In other words, the *need* is for the intimacy that comes with sharing vulnerability and exploring something new together, and the way Alex *wants* to do that is through anal play. Perhaps Alex identifies that the core feature of the fantasy is the actual sensation that accompanies anal stimulation. Then the *need* is experiencing that stimulation, while the *want* is to engage in whichever type of stimulation Alex is looking for in the presence of or by Jessie.

Once Alex has done all this hard work, the last step is simply to ask. Of course, there are an infinite number of ways to start a conversation like this. Keeping the guidelines in mind, Alex may choose to say something like:

ALEX: Jessie, I'd like to chat about some ideas I have about our sex life. Is now a good time, or should we talk later?

The important features of Alex's query are asking permission and letting Jessie know that the conversation will be about sex. Also, Alex is rolling this topic out casually rather than filled with trepidation. Remember, making a request is an opportunity to enhance our sexual well-being; it is not a burden or barrier to it.

Let's suppose that Alex and Jessie find a time to talk, and Alex has told Jessie about wanting to explore anal play. Now, Jessie is receiving a request. Jessie's most important job as the receiver of the request is to stay calm. Alex is being vulnerable and courageous by making a request; it requires a tremendous amount of trust to be so open. By making this request, Alex is showing Jessie that there is a great deal of love and trust in this relationship. Jessie, in turn, should love Alex back by receiving the request calmly and nonjudgmentally. This is just an initial conversation between Alex and Jessie—a preliminary exchange of information. No decisions need to be made, and no consent needs to be given at the end of this conversation. All that is happening is that Alex is giving Jessie information. Jessie can respond in several ways. Depending on how Jessie feels, the conversation can go in several directions. Let's explore some possibilities.

Scenario A:

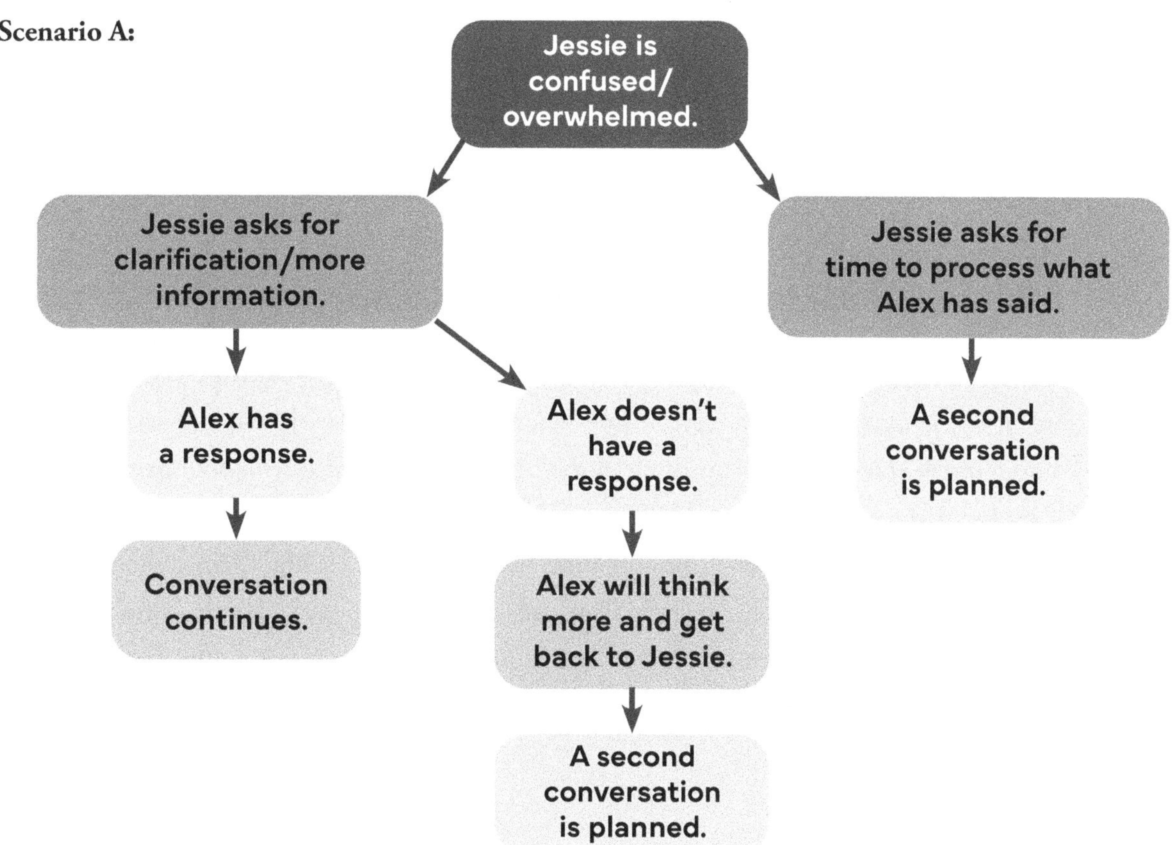

Scenario B:

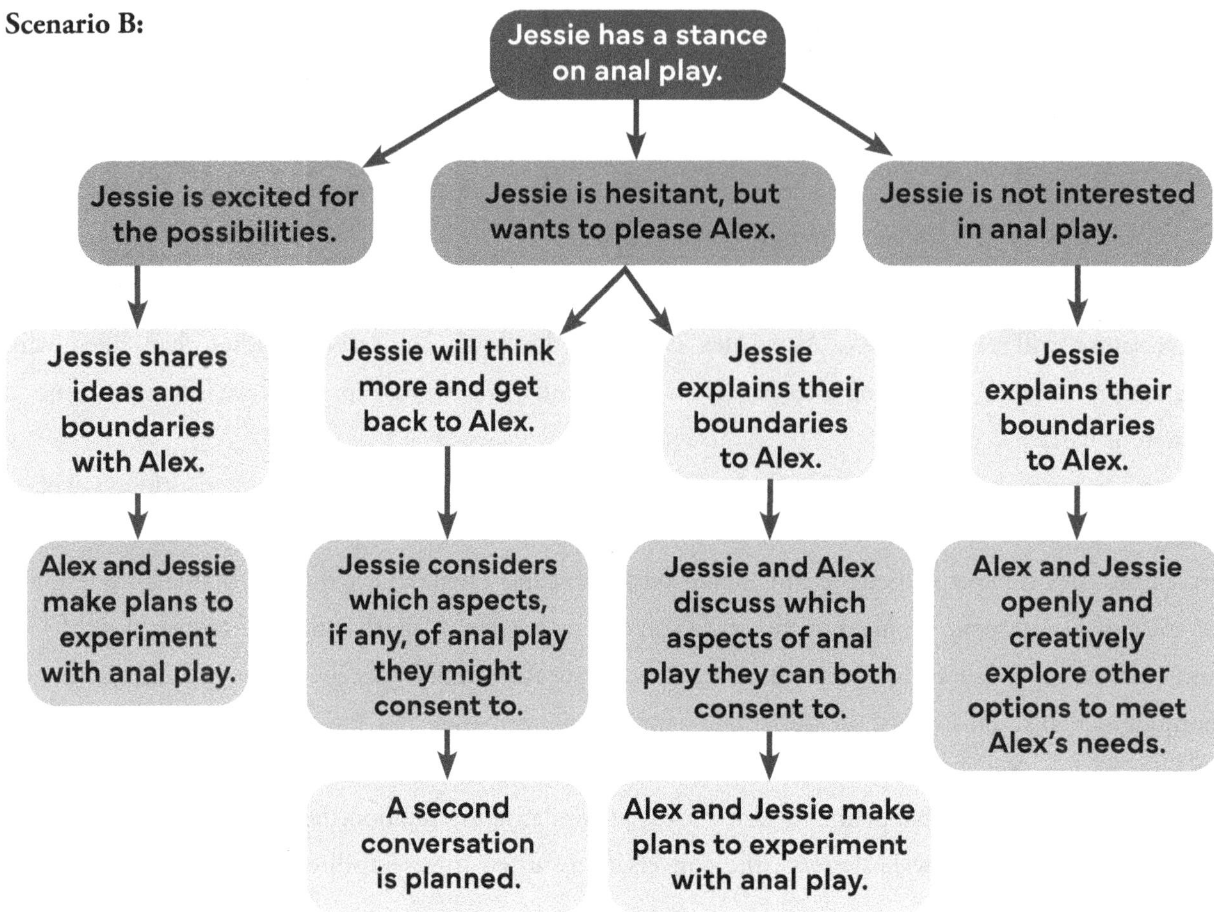

Notice some of the features of both these scenarios. Most paths lead to having a second conversation, and perhaps a third, and a fourth. Because sexuality is complex, finding common ground can take quite a while. Push your clients to stay patient and open and they will get there in time.

Setting or Receiving a Boundary

In the flow charts in the previous section, there is mention of identifying boundaries. As you read in chapters 4 and 5, a boundary is a metaphorical line that we cannot cross without the relationship or scenario becoming unsafe. Have your clients think of their boundaries as the instruction manual for how they stay safe and healthy in relationships with other people. For example, if a client has a friend or family member that comes to them for emotional support time and time again, leaving them feeling depleted, they might need to set a boundary. Perhaps the client can communicate with them less frequently, or tell them that they can only talk for ten minutes at a time. Such a decision is not a punishment for bad behavior. Instead, it allows them to sustain a relationship with that person without feeling depleted and resentful.

Boundaries are vital to true consent. After all, how can we trust that a yes is a yes, if we never hear a no? When it comes to sex, boundaries are what allow your clients to experiment and explore without the danger of the scenario becoming unsafe. Knowing the boundaries of each partner and encouraging them to express those boundaries to one another is what allows them to have great, satisfying sex. In short, learn to love boundaries, and teach your clients to love them, too.

The first step to setting boundaries is to identify them. Perhaps your clients have clarity around certain things that they absolutely do not want to do. Excellent! These are called *hard boundaries*. A hard boundary is a very clear "no," and it is not subject to negotiation. In other words, there is almost no scenario in which that particular act is acceptable for your client. Keep in mind that if they set a hard boundary now but something changes in the future, they are absolutely allowed to revisit it. In this situation, it is only the person who set the boundary that is allowed to bring it up for reassessment.

Hard boundaries tend to be the more obvious ones—things that your clients are opposed to, turned off by, or fearful of. *Soft boundaries* are a bit trickier. These are the things that we are unsure of but not necessarily opposed to. Perhaps there is something that your clients have fantasized about, but they are unsure whether or not their partner will enjoy it in real life. Maybe there is something that is not one partner's cup of tea, but it is perfectly acceptable to them should it be something that their partner is very interested in. These are soft boundaries—they are flexible, but it's not quite set on *how* flexible they are. It's important that your clients communicate to their partner that something is a soft boundary, because exploration of it, both verbal and physical, requires proper caution, privileging of consent, and care for each partner's experience.

In the previous section, Alex and Jessie began a conversation about incorporating anal play into their sex life together. With the exception of ending the conversation due to overwhelm, all options incorporate some explanation of boundaries. Even if Alex and Jessie are both interested in anal play, that does not mean that they are both equally interested in all potential aspects of it. Perhaps Alex wants to be penetrated, but Jessie does not. They should both know this before embarking on any sort of physical exploration.

There is one potential response that deserves more attention: Jessie is hesitant but wants to please Alex. This is a common scenario when talking about sexual wants and needs. Please note that someone wanting to please their partner is 1) *not* consent and 2) *not* a good enough reason to do something that they do not want to do. Often, people put pressure on themselves to anticipate and fulfill the desires of their partner for fear of infidelity or breaking up. To be clear, setting a boundary does not cause either of these events. The dissolution of fidelity or a relationship requires an active choice. While it is true that some people decide to end their relationships after realizing that it is not possible to be adequately satisfied in that relationship, this choice is the result of much communication and consideration, not a single instance of setting a boundary. While it is also true that sexual incompatibility makes relationships difficult, they do not need to end because one desire was not able to be fulfilled. Healthy relationships can bend and flex to accommodate a wide variety (though not all) of disparate needs, both met and unmet, of the parties involved.

Jessie's work regarding this conversation is to get a sense of their own hard and soft boundaries. Jessie may be interested in trying something that they have never tried before, but they don't know if they will like it or not. Communicating their soft boundaries is important because it clues Alex into moments or acts that they should be cautious around or pay extra attention to. Some people use a traffic light as a metaphor for sexual boundaries—green means go (yes), red means stop (no), and yellow means proceed with caution.

When Jessie sets boundaries with Alex, both partners must respect the boundaries. This means that Alex does not try to go beyond the boundary while interacting with Jessie, and Jessie does not remove a boundary while interacting with Alex. Boundaries should not change during a sexual interaction, but that does not mean they can't ever change.

Reflecting on Sexual Exploration

This brings us to the last step of sexual exploration. Let's say that Alex and Jessie successfully discussed, planned, and engaged in a sexual interaction involving anal play. Now it's time to reflect on that experience together. What did they each like, not like, or wish was different? Had the interaction been what either of them expected? What do they want to do again? Is there a direction that they would like to explore further?

Importantly, Alex and Jessie need to revisit the issue of boundaries. Having had this experience together, has anything changed for either of them? Are any yellow lights now green or red? Were there any events that occurred that neither of them had anticipated but that they must now discuss? Boundaries evolve and change over time, so boundary conversations must be ongoing and revisited.

Now, let's suppose that Alex and Jessie's interaction did not go well. Alex, in the heat of the moment, tried something with Jessie that Jessie did not consent to. Jessie began to feel unsafe and stopped the encounter. Both Alex and Jessie are now upset. Before they can debrief and reflect on the experience, they need to reestablish their connection. Perhaps they hug, apologize, or share an intimate joke—something specific to their relationship that helps them feel connected to each other. When they are both ready to talk about what happened, they can discuss what took place, what about it hurt, and how they can prevent the situation from being repeated.

Client Handout

Practicing Sexual Communication

Think about your sex life. What do you wish your partner knew about your sexual satisfaction? What would improve your satisfaction? Pick one thing to talk to your partner about. Ideally, choose a topic that has value but is not the most important thing to you. This is practice, after all. Decide how you will connect at the end of the activity (e.g., hug, watch a show) before embarking on it. Choose which of you will speak first, and follow these steps.

Speaker:

1. Identify what you want to do: express a concern, make a request, or set a boundary.
2. Ask permission to talk to your partner about it.
3. Be specific and clear in your communication; remember to use I-statements.
4. Ask for your partner's initial thoughts.
5. With your partner, decide when to discuss the topic again.

Listener:

1. Listen to your partner calmly.
2. Ask for clarifying or additional information if needed.
3. Form a nonjudgmental response. If you are aware of where your boundaries are already, state them. If not, ask for time to process this new information.
4. With your partner, decide when to discuss the topic again.

Now, switch roles and repeat the exercise. Be sure to end the exercise with your prearranged activity.

Practicing Sexual Communication Debrief

Ask your clients to share what it was like to be so open and vulnerable with their partner. How did it feel to have their partner listen and respond calmly? What was it like to experience their partner trusting them enough to be honest? How did this conversation differ from previous conversations that they have had about sex?

CHAPTER 10

Specific Topics in Sex Therapy

This chapter will touch on further specific topics in sex therapy. It would be impossible to cover all possible topics that you may encounter when talking with couples about sex, as well as all possible aspects of the topics you may discuss, so we have chosen to cover some common subjects that arise in sex therapy.* Here, you will learn briefly about various diagnoses related to sexuality, aging, disability, illness, procreation, pregnancy, the postpartum period, ethical non-monogamy, BDSM, kink, and sex work. It is important that you maintain a sex-positive stance when discussing these and other topics related to sexuality in therapy sessions. It's not just about the challenging stuff—it's also about the great stuff!

Diagnosis

The *Diagnostic and Statistical Manual of Mental Disorders, Fifth Edition* (*DSM-5*) has 19 diagnoses related to sexuality. It is important to note that these diagnoses contribute to the medicalization and pathologizing of sexual issues with their use of function versus dysfunction and normal versus abnormal frameworks. Thus, diagnosis of sexual functioning flies in the face of sex positivity. Nevertheless, depending on how you practice, diagnosis may be an important aspect of your work, particularly when it comes to reimbursement from insurance companies.

> *As a side note, if you are using a sexual functioning diagnosis for insurance purposes, make sure that your clients' plans actually cover that diagnosis as a primary diagnosis, as many plans do not.*

The *DSM-5* splits sexual functioning diagnoses into the categories of sexual dysfunction and paraphilic disorders. The sexual functioning category contains disorders of arousal (female sexual interest/arousal disorder and male hypoactive sexual desire disorder), ejaculation (premature ejaculation and delayed ejaculation), erectile disorder, female orgasmic disorder, and genito-pelvic pain/penetration

* Abuse and infidelity, as mentioned previously in this book, are also common issues in sex therapy. Return to chapter 6 anytime you need to review this information.

disorder. These disorders can be specified as lifelong or acquired; generalized or situational; and mild, moderate, or severe. In addition, this category also includes other specified sexual dysfunction and unspecified sexual dysfunction. The paraphilic disorders include eight specific disorders (voyeuristic, exhibitionistic, frotteuristic, sexual masochism, sexual sadism, pedophilic, fetishistic, and transvestic) as well as other specified paraphilic disorder and unspecified paraphilic disorder. The criteria for all of these are outlined in the *DSM-5* (American Psychiatric Association, 2013).

Procreation, Pregnancy, and Postpartum

While not all couples have sex for procreational purposes, many do. The transition from a recreational activity to a procreational activity can really throw some couples for a loop. Often, couples will voice that the spontaneity and magic are gone and that it is difficult to have sex on demand. When working with such couples, it is important to be sensitive to their sense of loss regarding the sex life they are used to having as well as their fear that it won't return. In addition, the process of trying to get pregnant also challenges many clients' relationships with their bodies and partners. Feelings of guilt, resentment, betrayal, and shame can emerge during the journey of trying to conceive, particularly if it is a difficult process or involves medical intervention.

Everyone's experience of pregnancy is unique to them, and you should not make assumptions about how your clients relate to their pregnancy. Make sure to ask broad, open-ended questions to get a sense of how your clients are feeling. Most often, though not always, one partner is pregnant while the other is not. Sometimes, this is a difficult asymmetry that results in feelings of resentment on the pregnant partner's side, and feelings of helplessness on the non-pregnant partner's side. With regard to sex, people's reactions to pregnancy are widely varied. Some people feel too ill and tired to engage sexually, others become more easily aroused and interested in sex, and for still others, sex is simply the last thing on their mind. In the later stages of pregnancy, mobility may become more of a challenge, and your clients will need to get creative about positioning themselves and using props. Lastly, it is important to note that, due to the multitude of physical changes that take place during and after pregnancy, the pregnant client may find that new areas of their body have become more or less sensitive to touch. If your clients are up for it, this is a great opportunity for exploration.

Postpartum, like pregnancy, is a unique experience that often changes the way a person relates to their body. Sometimes this relationship with self will return to the way it was pre-baby, and other times, it is more of a permanent change. Often, this is a time of decreased frequency of sex for couples due to the stress of having an infant, a lack of sleep, and a changing of daily schedules. Additionally, if the person giving birth chooses to breastfeed, there can even be a sense that their body is no longer their own, and it is very difficult for some couples to navigate the transition between a body being a vessel for pleasure and a body being a vessel for life.

Aging

Aging often presents physical challenges to a couple's sex life. Changes in hormone levels often lead to more difficulty with getting and maintaining erections. This may require couples to be more planful around sex and creatively fluid around the activities that they engage in. Furthermore, hormonal changes result in the thinning of vaginal tissue and a decrease in self-lubrication. Because of these changes, additional lubrication and adequate foreplay may be required for any sort of penetrative sex. In addition, orgasm may become harder to achieve. This is an excellent time to shift your couple's definition of a "successful sexual encounter" from orgasm to pleasure and connectedness.

Mobility and cardiovascular issues may also present in older populations. It is important to remind your couples that acrobatic sex is not required for a fulfilling sex life. Finding positions that are not painful (or minimally painful) for each partner is vital. Also, slowing down the pace of sexual behavior may be important, as well as the use of props such as pillows, foam wedges, and slings. As you discuss these functional changes and the couple's feelings about them, be sure to highlight that they can add a fun new dimension to the couple's encounters.

Disability and Illness

Much like aging, disability and illness present additional considerations for having sex—enough that this section could be its own book! In fact, there are several books on these matters. (Check out *The Ultimate Guide to Sex and Disability* by Miriam Kaufman, Cory Silverberg, and Fran Odette; and *Sex When You're Sick* by Anne Katz.)

When working with clients who live with disabilities or illness, it is important to understand both the limits of their capacity and the consequences for exceeding that capacity (e.g., immobility, spasms, fatigue, pain). It is up to the client, not you, to decide how they would like to manage their capacity. For example, a common misconception is that if something hurts, we should never do it. But what if everything hurts? While it would be fine for a client to choose to not be sexual, most clients will not want to go in this direction. Therefore, discussions should focus around lessening pain and mitigating consequences rather than focusing on how to partake with no pain at all. For clients who live with disabilities, conversations should center around whatever is available with regard to movement and sensation. Most sex toys, for example, are not made with disabilities in mind. You and your clients may have to employ some creativity to figure out how to meet their sexual goals.

Ethical Non-Monogamy

As we discussed in chapter 6, ethical non-monogamy (ENM) is the practice of having sexual and romantic relationships with more than one person at a time. It is based on the belief that a person can engage in multiple satisfying relationships and that sexual exclusivity is not the gold standard for commitment in a relationship. ENM can take many forms, and it is important to let your clients define their own version of ENM. Not only are there an infinite number of ENM structures, but partners also vary in how much they want to know about or be involved with their partner's other relationships.

In ENM relationships, you will deal with balancing the sexual needs of each partner, however many there may be. Sexual health tends to be a topic of conversation, as the behavior of one partner can affect the health of both them and their other partners. It is important to discuss safer sex practices, including regular STI testing and the use of (or lack of) physical barriers, such as condoms, and hormonal barriers, such as oral contraceptives.

BDSM and Kink

Like ENM, when it comes to BDSM (bondage/discipline, domination/submission, sadism, and masochism) and kink (sexual practices, interests, concepts, or fantasies that are outside of the sexual practices narrowly defined by mainstream culture and media), the possibilities are infinite. It would be impossible to address every topic that could potentially fall under these wide umbrellas, but it is important to note that any kind of engagement in BDSM or kink play is very vulnerable and often leads to intense intimacy between partners.

Generally speaking, when it comes to exploring BDSM and kink, the two most important factors are *consent* and *safety*. Within certain types of bondage/discipline or domination/submission relationship dynamics, verbal communication may not be an option; this requires couples to plan how they are going to communicate consent and withdrawal of consent during a scene if they are not able or allowed to speak or move certain body parts. Similarly, some sexual practices may present additional health risks, such as breath play (e.g., choking, gagging, or otherwise restricting the flow of breath) or food fetishes (which can bring increased risk of infection). It is important to make sure that your couples are playing as safely as they can by making them aware of the increased risks involved in their particular play, ensuring communication around safety signals, and reviewing how to best mitigate inherent risks. Educating your clients on physical and emotional safety is an excellent way to support and affirm their sexual interests. To review the basics of consent and safety in relationships, see chapter 9.

BDSM play, in particular, can be very intense, and it's important to reestablish connection afterward; this is known as *aftercare*. You want to make sure that your clients are taking the time to address their aftercare needs. Common aftercare techniques include hugging, cuddling, and discussing the events that just took place (e.g., what was good, what wasn't so good).

Sex Work

Over the course of working with couples, you may discover that one or more of them have engaged in or is engaging in sex work. This line of work has some serious stigma attached to it. It is vital that you check and work through your own biases around sex work. Not only is this process essential to your ability to work with clients, but you may have to help one or more of them do the same thing, especially if sex work comes out as a secret during the treatment.

In addition to wading through the stigma and myths that surround sex work, you will need to discuss safer sex practices with clients. Assuming that one or both of your clients will continue to do this work, their relationship should be treated much the same way as an ENM relationship structure. Because the behavior of one partner affects the health of all potential partners, it is important to discuss regular STI testing as well as physical and hormonal contraception.

CHAPTER 11

Continuing Your Journey

This book has covered a variety of topics related to sex therapy and couples therapy. By now, you should feel like you've dipped your toe into the pools of both. You've learned about what makes couples work different from individual work, and you've had a brief overview of the theories related to couples and sex therapy. You should also be able to explain the role of attachment styles in conflict and identify negative cycles of relationship conflict.

In addition, you now understand emotional regulation and why it is a key relationship skill. You've learned how conflicts escalate and are maintained, as well as how to de-escalate and repair ruptures. Furthermore, you've delved into common presenting problems in couples work.

You are now able to answer the question: *Why is sex important*? You understand the benefits of sex and the importance of sex positivity. You've investigated desire and arousal, and you understand how the dual-control model and concordant and discordant arousal work. Moreover, you've learned helpful guidelines for communicating around sex intimacy, and you've briefly covered some specific topics that arise in sex therapy.

You have done all of this incredible work throughout the book, but, since it's only an introduction to this work, you may be wondering, what else is there? Perhaps this book has left you with more questions than you had to begin with. Where can you go to continue building your skills?

Supervision

As with all areas of burgeoning competence in therapy, supervision is essential. Whether you are seeking individual supervision or group supervision, it is important that you seek out a qualified supervisor. This means a supervisor who has extensive experience in couples therapy, either generally or in a specific orientation, and who has trained specifically as a supervisor.

The following are helpful questions to ask potential supervisors:

- What are your credentials?
- How long have you been practicing couples or sex therapy?

- How long have you been supervising therapists?
- Do you have formal training in supervision?
- What is your supervision style (e.g., didactic, collaborative)?
- What orientation do you use in your practice, or do you take an eclectic approach?
- Are there certain areas or issues that you do not work with? If so, which ones and why?

For supervision in treating specific couples therapy orientations, you can visit the websites of their official organizations to find a trained supervisor—for example, you can go to the International Centre for Excellence in Emotionally Focused Therapy's (ICEEFT) website to find a certified supervisor for EFT (https://iceeft.com). For sex therapy, you can pursue individual and group supervision with a supervisor certified by the American Association of Sexuality Educators, Counselors, and Therapists (AASECT; https://www.aasect.org).

Although many therapists find reviewing tapes of their work anxiety-provoking, supervision is very helpful when you are able to do so. (Note: This requires you to get a signed release from your clients to record your sessions for review in supervision.) A good supervisor will encourage you to pursue recording your work and will also be understanding of any anxiety you may experience when showing your work to them. Rewatching sessions with a trained supervisor can help you quickly identify strengths, mistakes, and areas for continued improvement in your work. The unavoidable truth is that to become the best couple therapist you can be, as efficiently as possible, you need to get comfortable with assessing your work. This doesn't mean criticizing yourself; it means analyzing your sessions with a clinical eye for how you can continue to improve as a clinician.

Additional Training and Certification Paths

As you know from chapter 2, there are numerous evidence-based orientations for working with couples. When considering additional trainings to pursue, the first thing to consider is going "to the source." For example, if you're interested in learning more about Gottman Method couples therapy, you can go directly to the Gottman Institute to find trainings. Therapists can also explore different orientations and methods through companies that offer clinician-focused education. This can be a great place to start when you want to gain a breadth of knowledge before diving deeper into a specific theoretical orientation and practice, or if you want to continue pursuing general couples or sex therapy training without committing to one orientation.

Along with additional trainings, you can pursue certification in a specific type of couples or sex therapy. This may make sense once you have learned more about the various approaches and decided which one resonates most with your clinical style. The benefit of certification is that you'll gain undeniable proficiency in that modality, and prospective clients will know you are qualified to treat couples. Each certification process is different, but they typically require several formal trainings, supervision, and review of your clinical work. To learn more, you can look into the specific orientation's certification track. For example, clinicians can go to the ICEEFT for EFT certification or The Gottman Institute for Gottman certification.

> *Not all types of couples therapy have certification tracks or even official organizations that represent them. For example, there are many training offerings for integrative cognitive behavioral therapy, but there isn't a specific certification. For these modalities, you will need to use your judgment when selecting courses to further your education. Seeking training from well-established companies or qualified professors is recommended.*

AASECT is the governing body of sex therapy certification in the United States. While it is possible to cobble together the requirements for certification through workshops, conferences, and continuing education, it is recommended that you complete a program designed specifically for the certification. Depending on your preferred format, time, money constraints, and location, you may consider programs through the following avenues: University of Michigan, South Shore Sexual Health Center, Sexual Health Alliance, Modern Sex Therapy Institutes, and Widener University.

Continued Reading

Along with pursuing supervision, additional training, or certification, you can continue your learning through reading on your own. There are many excellent books about all aspects of couples therapy and sex therapy that can help you deepen your understanding of the work. The list below is not exhaustive, but it is a good starting point for self-education.

Recommended Books

- *After the Affair: Healing the Pain and Rebuilding Trust When a Partner Has Been Unfaithful* by Janis A. Spring
- *Come As You Are: The Surprising New Science That Will Transform Your Sex Life* by Emily Nagoski
- *Come Together: The Science (and Art!) of Creating Lasting Sexual Connections* by Emily Nagoski
- *The Ethical Slut: A Practical Guide to Polyamory, Open Relationships & Other Adventures* by Dossie Easton and Janet Hardy
- *Facing Codependence: What It Is, Where It Comes from, How It Sabotages Our Lives* by Pia Mellody
- *Guide to Getting It On* by Paul Joannides

- *Helping Couples on the Brink of Divorce: Discernment Counseling for Troubled Relationships* by William J. Doherty and Steven M. Harris
- *Hold Me Tight: Seven Conversations for a Lifetime of Love* by Sue Johnson
- *Mating in Captivity: Unlocking Erotic Intelligence* by Esther Perel
- *New Directions in Sex Therapy: Innovations and Alternatives* (2nd ed.) by Peggy Kleinplatz
- *Opening Up: A Guide to Creating and Sustaining Open Relationships* by Tristan Taormino
- *Polysecure: Attachment, Trauma and Consensual Nonmonogamy* by Jessica Fern
- *Principles and Practice of Sex Therapy* (6th ed.), edited by Kathryn S. K. Hall and Yitzchak M. Binik
- *Queer Sex: A Trans and Non-Binary Guide to Intimacy, Pleasure, and Relationships* by Juno Roche
- *The Relationship Cure: A 5 Step Guide to Strengthening Your Marriage, Family, and Friendships* by John M. Gottman and Joan DeClaire
- *Secure Love: Create a Relationship that Lasts a Lifetime* by Julie Mennano
- *The Seven Principles for Making Marriage Work* by John M. Gottman and Nan Silver
- *Sex When You're Sick: Reclaiming Sexual Health after Illness or Injury* by Anne Katz
- *The Ultimate Guide to Sex and Disability: For All of Us Who Live with Disabilities, Chronic Pain, and Illness* by Miriam Kaufman, Cory Silverberg, and Fran Odette
- *Us: Getting Past You & Me to Build a More Loving Relationship* by Terry Real

Additional Resources

- Emily Nagoski's website (including free downloadable worksheets): https://www.emilynagoski.com/come-as-you-are-worksheets
- American Association of Sexuality Educators, Counselors, and Therapists: https://www.aasect.org
- The Gottman Institute: https://www.gottman.com/free-resources-for-professionals
- International Centre for Excellence in Emotionally Focused Therapy: https://iceeft.com/diversity-resources

Conclusion

Working with couples is a challenging but very fulfilling clinical niche. Sessions tend to be intense, fast-paced, and emotionally charged. We invite you to reflect on what sparked your desire to engage in this unique type of therapeutic work. Think about what you've learned from this book and how it will inform your practice. In what ways do you feel better prepared to work with this population? What barriers or biases have you identified? What do you need to learn more about so you feel competent and confident pursuing this work?

This book is just the start. As therapists, we are lifelong learners; there is no end to assessing and improving our work. Even we, as authors of a book about couples and sex therapy, are continuously seeking supervision, consultation, and additional training. Consider this book the start of a wonderful journey of learning, self-growth, and insight. We're grateful for your interest in pursuing this incredibly meaningful work, and we hope this book energizes you to continue your journey.

References

For your convenience, the practices in this book are available for download at www.pesi.com/navigatingintimacy

Ainsworth, M. D. S., Bell, S. M., & Stayton, D. J. (1971). Individual differences in strange-situation behavior of one-year-olds. In H. R. Schaffer (Ed.) *The origins of human social relations.* Academic Press.

Allan, R., & Johnson, S. M. (2017). Conceptual and application issues: Emotionally focused therapy with gay male couples. *Journal of Couple & Relationship Therapy, 16*(4), 286–305. https://doi.org/10.1080/15332691.2016.1238800

Allen, M. S. (2018). Sexual activity and cognitive decline in older adults. *Archives of Sexual Behavior, 47*(6), 1711–1719. https://doi.org/10.1007/s10508-018-1193-8

American Psychiatric Association. (2013). *Diagnostic and statistical manual of mental disorders* (5th ed.).

Annon, J. S. (1976). The PLISSIT model: A proposed conceptual scheme for the behavioral treatment of sexual problems. *Journal of Sex Education and Therapy, 2*(1), 1–15. https://doi.org/10.1080/01614576.1976.11074483

Bairstow, A. (2017). Couples exploring nonmonogamy: Guidelines for therapists. *Journal of Sex and Marital Therapy, 43*(4), 343–535. https://doi.org/10.1080/0092623X.2016.1164782

Bancroft, J., Graham, C. A., Janssen, E., & Sanders, S. A. (2009). The dual control model: Current status and future Directions. *Journal of Sex Research, 46*(2-3), 121–142. https://doi.org/10.1080/00224490902747222

Bass, B. A., & Quimby, J. L. (2006). Addressing secrets in couples counseling: An alternative approach to informed consent. *The Family Journal, 14*(1), 77–80. https://doi.org/10.1177/1066480705282060

Beasley, C. C., & Ager, R. (2019). Emotionally focused couples therapy: A systematic review of its effectiveness over the past 19 years. *Journal of Evidence-Based Social Work, 16*(2), 144–159. https://doi.org/10.1080/23761407.2018.1563013

Bowlby, J. (1969). *Attachment and loss.* Basic Books.

Bradford, A. B., Johnson, L. N., Anderson, S. R., Banford-Witting, A., Hunt, Q. A., Miller, R. B., & Bean, R. A. (2024). Call me maybe? In-person vs. teletherapy outcomes among married couples. *Psychotherapy Research, 34*(5), 611-625. https://doi.org/10.1080/10503307.2023.2256465

Catania, J. A. (2020). Dyadic sexual communication scale. In R. Milhausen (Ed.), *Handbook of sexuality-related measures* (4th ed., pp. 212–214). Routledge.

Debrot, A., Meuwly, N., Muise, A., Impett, E. A., & Schoebi, D. (2017). More than just sex: affection mediates the association between sexual activity and well-being. *Personality & Social Psychology Bulletin, 43*(3), 287–299. https://doi.org/10.1177/0146167216684124

Doherty, W. J. (2011). In or out: Treating the mixed-agenda couple. *Psychotherapy Networker, 35*(6), 45–60.

Doherty, W. J., & Harris, S. M. (2017). *Helping couples on the brink of divorce: Discernment counseling for troubled relationships.* American Psychological Association. https://doi.org/10.1037/0000029-000

Doherty, W. J., Harris, S. M., & Wilde, J. L. (2016). Discernment counseling for "mixed-agenda" couples. *Journal of Marital and Family Therapy, 42*(2), 246–255. https://doi.org/10.1111/jmft.12132

Doss, B. D., Roddy, M. K., Wiebe, S. A., & Johnson, S. M. (2022). A review of the research during 2010–2019 on evidence-based treatments for couple relationship distress. *Journal of Marital and Family Therapy, 48*(1), 283–306. https://doi.org/10.1111/jmft.12552

Edwards, C., Allan, R., Marzo, N., Wynfield, T., & Hicks, R. (2023). The use of emotionally focused therapy with polyamorous relationships. *Family Process, 62*(4), 1362–1376. https://doi.org/10.1111/famp.12934

Edwards, W. M., & Coleman, E. (2004). Defining sexual health: A descriptive overview. *Archives of Sexual Behavior, 33*(3), 189–195. https://doi.org/10.1023/B:ASEB.0000026619.95734.d5

Emerson, A. J., Harris, S. M., & Ahmed, F. A. (2021). The impact of discernment counseling on individuals who decide to divorce: Experiences of post-divorce communication and coparenting. *Journal of Marital and Family Therapy, 47*(1), 36–51. https://doi.org/10.1111/jmft.12463

Epstein, N. B., & Baucom, D. H. (2002). Cognitive and emotional factors in couples' relationships. In *Enhanced cognitive-behavioral therapy for couples: A contextual approach* (pp. 65–104). American Psychological Association. https://doi.org/10.1037/10481-003

Friedlander, M. L., Lambert, J. E., & de la Peña, C. M. (2008). A step toward disentangling the alliance/improvement cycle in family therapy. *Journal of Counseling Psychology, 55*(1), 118–124. https://doi.org/10.1037/0022-0167.55.1.118

Garanzini, S., Yee, A., Gottman, J., Gottman, J., Cole, C., Preciado, M., & Jasculca, C. (2017). Results of Gottman Method couples therapy with gay and lesbian couples. *Journal of Marital and Family Therapy, 43*(4), 674–684. https://doi.org/10.1111/jmft.12276

Gottman, J. M. (1993). A theory of marital dissolution and stability. *Journal of Family Psychology, 7*(1), 57–75. https://doi.org/10.1037/0893-3200.7.1.57

Gottman, J. M., & Gottman, J. S. (2008). Gottman method couple therapy. In A. S. Gurman (Ed.), *Clinical handbook of couple therapy* (4th ed., pp. 138–164). The Guilford Press.

Gottman, J. M., & Silver, N. (2012). *What makes love last?: How to build trust and avoid betrayal.* Simon & Schuster.

Gottman, J. M., & Silver, N. (2015). *The seven principles for making marriage work : A practical guide from the country's foremost relationship expert* (2nd ed.) Harmony.

Greenberg, L. S., & Johnson, S. M. (1988). *Emotionally focused therapy for couples.* Guilford Press.

Gurman, A. S., & Snyder, D. K. (2011). Couple therapy. In J. C. Norcross, G. R. VandenBos, & D. K. Freedheim (Eds.), *History of psychotherapy: Continuity and change* (2nd ed., pp. 485–496). American Psychological Association. https://doi.org/10.1037/12353-029

Hart, J. (2023). Harvard study of adult development: Human connection is key to health and well-being. *Integrative and Complementary Therapies, 29*(3), 122–124. https://doi.org/10.1089/ict.2023.29074.jha

Hendrix, H., Hunt, H., Luquet, W., and Carlson, J. (2015). Using the Imago dialogue to deepen couples therapy. *Journal of Individual Psychology 71*(3), 253–272.

Hertlein, K. M., Weeks, G. R., & Sendak, S. K. (2009). *A clinician's guide to systemic sex therapy.* Routledge.

Hooper, A., Spann, C., McCray, T., & Kimberly, C. (2017). Revisiting the basics: Understanding potential demographic differences with John Gottman's Four Horsemen and emotional flooding. *The Family Journal, 25*(3), 224–229. https://doi.org/10.1177/1066480717710650

Irvine T. J., & Peluso P. R. (2022). An affair to remember: A mixed-methods survey examining therapists' experiences treating infidelity. *The Family Journal, 30*(3), 324–333. https://doi.org/10.1177/10664807211061826

Jacobson, N. S., & Christensen, A. (1996). *Integrative behavioral couple therapy: Promoting acceptance and change.* W. W. Norton.

Johnson, S., & Brubacher, L. (2016). Clarifying the negative cycle in emotionally focused couple therapy (EFT). In G. R. Weeks, S. T. Fife, & C. M. Peterson (Eds.), *Techniques for the couple therapist: Essential interventions from the experts.* (pp. 92–96). Routledge.

Kaplan, H. S. (1974). *The new sex therapy: Active treatment of sexual dysfunctions.* Brunner/Mazel.

Kirkpatrick, L. A., & Hazan, C. (1994). Attachment styles and close relationships: A four-year prospective study. *Personal Relationships, 1*(2), 123–142. https://doi.org/10.1111/j.1475-6811.1994.tb00058.x

Kisler, T. S., & Lock, L. (2019). Honoring the voices of polyamorous clients: Recommendations for couple and family therapists. *Journal of Feminist Family Therapy, 31*(1), 40–58. https://doi.org/10.1080/08952833.2018.1561017

Kleinplatz, P. J., Ménard, A. D., Paquet, M.-P., Paradis, N., Campbell, M., Zuccarino, D., & Mehak, L. (2009). The components of optimal sexuality: A portrait of "great sex." *Canadian Journal of Human Sexuality, 18*(1–2), 1–13.

Kuo, F.-C. (2009). Secrets or no secrets: Confidentiality in couple therapy. *American Journal of Family Therapy, 37*(5), 351–354. https://doi.org/10.1080/01926180701862970

Levine, E. C., Herbenick, D., Martinez, O., Fu, T.-C., & Dodge, B. (2018). Open relationships, nonconsensual nonmonogamy, and monogamy among U.S. adults: Findings from the 2012 National Survey of Sexual Health and Behavior. *Archives of Sexual Behavior, 47*(5), 1439–1450. https://doi.org/10.1007/s10508-018-1178-7

Liu, H., Waite, L. J., Shen, S., & Wang, D. H. (2016). Is sex good for your health? A national study on partnered sexuality and cardiovascular risk among older men and women. *Journal of Health and Social Behavior, 57*(3), 276–296. https://doi.org/10.1177/0022146516661597

Mark, K. P., & Schuman, D. L. (2020). A scoping review of the practice recommendations of secrets in couple's therapy. *Journal of Family Psychotherapy, 31*(1–2), 56–71. https://doi.org/10.1080/08975353.2020.1759019

Masters, W. H., & Johnson, V. E. (1970). *Human sexual inadequacy.* Little, Brown, and Company.

McCarthy, B. W., & Metz, M. E. (2012). The Good-Enough Sex (GES) model. In P. J. Kleinplatz (Ed.), *New directions in sex therapy: Innovations and alternatives* (2nd ed., pp. 213–229). Routledge/Taylor & Francis Group.

Meston, C. M., Stanton, A. M., & Buss, D. M. (2020). The why have sex questionnaire. In R. R. Milhausen, J. K. Sakaluk, T. D., Fisher, C. M. Davis, & W. L. Yarber (Eds.), *Handbook of sexuality-related measures* (4th ed., p. 473). Routledge.

Money, J. (1988). Commentary: Current status of sex research. *Journal of Psychology and Human Sexuality, 1,* 5–16.

Moors, A. C. (2023). Five misconceptions about consensually nonmonogamous relationships. *Current Directions in Psychological Science, 32*(5), 355–361. https://doi.org/10.1177/09637214231166853

Nagoski, E. (2015). *Come as you are: The surprising new science that will transform your sex life.* Simon & Schuster.

Perel, E. (2017). *The state of affairs: Rethinking infidelity.* HarperCollins.

Pinsof, W. M., & Catherall, D. R. (1986). The integrative psychotherapy alliance: Family, couple and individual therapy scales. *Journal of Marital and Family Therapy, 12*(2), 137–151. https://doi.org/10.1111/j.1752-0606.1986.tb01631.x

Real, T. (2008). *The new rules of marriage: What you need to know to make love work.* Ballantine Books.

Real, T. (2022). *Us: Getting past you and me to build a more loving relationship.* Goop Press.

Rogers, P. (2018, October 18). The health benefits of sex. *Healthline.* Retrieved September 19, 2022, from https://www.healthline.com/health/healthy-sex-health-benefits

Roisman, G. L., Padrón, E., Sroufe, L. A., & Egeland, B. (2002). Earned-secure attachment status in retrospect and prospect. *Child Development, 73*(4), 1204–1219. https://doi.org/10.1111/1467-8624.00467

Safran, J. D., & Muran, J. C. (1996). The resolution of ruptures in the therapeutic alliance. *Journal of Consulting and Clinical Psychology, 64*(3), 447–458. https://doi.org/10.1037/0022-006X.64.3.447

Safran, J. D., & Muran, J. C. (2006). Has the concept of the therapeutic alliance outlived its usefulness? *Psychotherapy: Theory, Research, Practice, Training, 43*(3): 286–291. https://doi.org/10.1037/0033-3204.43.3.286

Snyder, D. K. (1999). Affective reconstruction in the context of a pluralistic approach to couple therapy. *Clinical Psychology: Science and Practice, 6*, 348-365.

Snyder, T. A., & Barnett, J. E. (2006). Informed consent and the psychotherapy process. *Psychotherapy Bulletin, 41*(2), 37–42. https://societyforpsychotherapy.org/wp-content/uploads/2018/07/2006-Psychotherapy-Bulletin-Volume-41-Number-2.pdf

Spring, J. A., & Spring, M. (1996). *After the affair: Healing the pain and rebuilding trust when a partner has been unfaithful.* HarperCollins.

Stuart, R. B. (1969). Operant-interpersonal treatment for marital discord. *Journal of Consulting and Clinical Psychology, 33*(6), 675–682. https://doi.org/10.1037/h0028475

Swank, L. E., & Wittenborn, A. K. (2013). Repairing alliance ruptures in emotionally focused couple therapy: A preliminary task analysis. *American Journal of Family Therapy, 41*(5), 389–402. https://doi.org/10.1080/01926187.2012.726595

Tilden, T., Johnson, S. U., Hoffart, A., Zahl-Olsen, R., Wampold, B. E., Ulvenes, P., & Håland, Å. T. (2021). Alliance predicting progress in couple therapy. *Psychotherapy, 58*(3), 391–400. https://doi.org/10.1037/pst0000355

Walker, L. E. (2005). The battered woman. In R. L. Kennedy Bergen, J. L. Edleson, & C. M. Renzetti (Eds.), *Violence against women: Classic papers* (pp. 220–228). Pearson Education New Zealand. (Reprinted from *The battered woman* by L. E. Walker, 1979, Harper and Row)

Wang, W. (2018). Who cheats more? The demographics of infidelity in America. *Institute for Family Studies*. https://ifstudies.org/blog/who-cheats-more-the-demographics-of-cheating-in-america

Wiebe, S. A., & Johnson, S. M. (2016). A review of the research in emotionally focused therapy for couples. *Family Process, 55*(3), 390–407. https://doi.org/10.1111/famp.12229

Zuccarini, D., & Karos, L. (2011). Emotionally focused therapy for gay and lesbian couples: Strong identities, strong bonds. In J. L. Furrow, S. M. Johnson, & B. A. Bradley (Eds.), *The emotionally focused casebook: New directions in treating couples.* (pp. 317–342). Routledge/Taylor & Francis Group.

Acknowledgments

Jointly, we would like to acknowledge our alma mater, William James College (although it will always be MSPP to us), its longtime president, Nick Covino, for supporting our project, and Julia Clement, for granting us library access. We'd like to thank William James for starting us on our career journeys in the field of clinical psychology, and for fortuitously putting us in classes together so that we could meet and form not only our collegial relationship but, more importantly, our friendship.

We are deeply grateful for Kayla Church and Chelsea Thompson at PESI Publishing. You have been wonderful to work with and we're so glad we could share this book with the world through your publishing house.

To Katherine Chase, thank you for your incredible support and love both for us and this project. We know how lucky we are to have you in our corner.

And we want to acknowledge the countless couples we have worked with over the years. You have trusted us, and we do not take that lightly. We are honored to have walked with you on your path toward happiness and health.

I, Dr. Isabelle Morley, want to thank my parents, Anne and Robert Eccles, for always supporting and encouraging me. You two have shown me that anything is possible with the right combination of dreaming, consistent hard work, and an unrestrained belief in oneself. I also want to thank my in-laws, Sylvia Balderrama and John Morley, for the constant love and support, and for watching my kids so that I could hole up in a coffee shop and write.

I wouldn't be where I am without the amazing professors and mentors who have taught me, challenged me, and cheered me. In particular, I'd like to thank my godmother Andrea Celenza, a fellow psychologist and truly talented author, who has been a guiding light throughout my career and continues to inspire me. I am grateful to have your footsteps to follow. I also want to extend my utmost gratitude to my EFT mentor, Deb Curtis. Deb, you spark excitement and motivation for mastering the model and working with couples, and because of you, I seek constant growth in my clinical work. Thank you for helping me self-reflect and grow, all while being unbelievably kind and supportive.

I would like to extend an immeasurable thank you to my family. To my husband, Lucas Morley, thank you for being excited for my work, for watching the kids so I could write on weekends, and for always believing in me, even when I have outrageous ideas. I know how lucky I am to have found a partner who cares about my success and happiness, and who is willing to grow together as we navigate this ever-changing life. And to my daughters, Maple and Wilde, thank you for being my motivation, for your unwavering enthusiasm about life that inspires me daily, and for sleeping just late enough so that I could write every morning.

And finally, I want to acknowledge my coauthor. Bailey Hanek, what can I say? We met over ten years ago and I feel like our journey has only just begun. Your commitment to your work, to excelling and growing as a clinician, has always inspired me. I'm grateful to have you as a colleague and, even more than that, as my friend. I'm beyond grateful for your unwavering presence in my life.

I, Dr. Bailey Hanek, would foremost like to acknowledge Michele Wall and Robert Hanek, who have listened to (and read) countless hours of me talking about this project. Their relentless support, encouragement, and involvement buoyed me along the way and kept my heart strong. Another thank you goes to Robin Wall Kimmerer, for her offers to hear my cries, and to Barbara Wall, for believing in my spirit . . . and for the snacks!

To those who have been along for my sex therapy education journey, I cannot thank you enough. To Sallie Foley and Valerie Wood, you created a home for people like me, nurtured me, and guided me. I could not have even dreamt of this book without you. To Jill Gracely, Lauren Briet, Sara Champine, and Tom Doctor—I hope you know what you've done for me, because words cannot express what you mean to me.

A big thank you to Lauren Morocco for her generous offers of support, time, and thoughtfulness. (Isabelle seconds this!).

To Lucas Morley, thank you for creating space for Isabelle to work with me. To Maple and Wilde, thank you for letting Isabelle occasionally sleep.

And lastly, to Isabelle Morley, my writing partner and friend. We started this journey together in 2011; little did we know that it would bring us here. Thank you for pushing me, guiding me, and loving me. I'm so thankful that we regularly express our gratitude to one another, otherwise this acknowledgment would be its own book. Thank you, thank you, thank you.

About the Authors

Isabelle Morley, PsyD, is a clinical psychologist and EFT-certified couples therapist (emotionally focused therapy). She is a contributing author to Psychology Today in her blog *Love Them or Leave Them*, where she analyzes on-screen romantic relationships. She is also the co-host of *Rom-Com Rescue*, a podcast that teaches life and love lessons from romantic comedies. Dr. Morley is frequently sought out by journalists for expert commentary on topics such as relationships, couples therapy, and reality television, and has been featured in *The New Yorker*, *The Boston Globe*, *Business Insider*, *Vox*, and *Verywell Mind*, among others. In philanthropic work, Dr. Morley is a founding board member of the Unscripted Cast Advocacy Network (UCAN) Foundation, a nonprofit organization that supports reality TV cast members in accessing mental health and legal support and advocates for industry change.

She received a bachelor of arts from Tufts University. As part of her major in peace and justice studies, she focused on interpersonal conflict resolution and wrote her capstone project on the evolutionary justification and modern-day use of forgiveness and revenge in relationships following significant transgressions. She earned her doctor of psychology degree from William James College in 2015. Her doctoral research explored young adults' perspectives on hookup culture and its impact on their ability to form meaningful romantic relationships. Dr. Morley started specializing in couples therapy early in her career, working with couples and pursuing additional education and training in many forms of couples therapy, including the Gottman Method, EFT, and relational life therapy. She worked at two group practices and served as a site director of a national mental health group before starting her private practice in 2021, where she provides therapy and intensives to couples. She lives and works in the Boston area.

Bailey Hanek, PsyD, is a licensed clinical psychologist, American Association of Sexuality Educators, Counselors, and Therapists (AASECT) certified sex therapist, and member of the American Psychological Association. In addition to her work with individuals and couples, she is a consultant and contributing author for the Between Us Clinic. Through this work, she has been quoted in popular publications, including *Men's Health* and *Mashable*, and developed a mindfulness program for low libido in men.

Dr. Hanek received her doctorate in clinical psychology from William James College in 2015. Her doctoral project focused on best practices for the use of sexually explicit media in sex therapy. Her internship and postdoctoral training spanned a range of populations and services, including psychodynamic assessment and treatment of adults at the Boston Institute for Psychotherapy; working with multi-stressed children and families through the family institute at YOU, Inc.; and psychological and neuropsychological testing with children through the assessment services branch of YOU, Inc. Following her licensure, Dr. Hanek joined the clinical staff at a group practice, where she provided therapy for adults and couples, as well as conducted psychological and neuropsychological testing for adults.

Currently, Dr. Hanek has her own practice in Cambridge, MA, where she provides general psychotherapy and sex therapy to an adult population, serving both individuals and couples. She offers both in-person and teletherapy options, as well as professional consultation.